Police Response to Mental Health Calls for Service

Policing Perspectives and Challenges in the Twenty-First Century

Series Editor: Jonathon A. Cooper, Indiana University of Pennsylvania

In many respects, policing has evolved over the last two centuries; yet issues that concerned policing in the nineteenth and twentieth centuries continue to be salient to contemporary law enforcement. But how these challenges are manifest to the police today are distinct, as society and politics, too, have evolved. And so understanding the role of police in society, the behavior and organization of law enforcement, the relationship between officers and civilians, and the intersection of theory and praxis remain important to the study of police. To this end, volumes in this series will consider policing perspectives and challenges in the twenty-first century, around the world, and through a variety of disciplinary lenses. Ultimately, this series "takes stock" of policing today, considers how it got here, and projects where it might be going. *Policing Perspectives and Challenges in the Twenty-First Century* will be of interest and use to a variety of policing scholars, including academics, police executives, and others who study law enforcement.

Titles in the series

Police Response to Mental Health Calls for Service

Gatekeepers and Street Corner Psychiatrists

Kayla G. Jachimowski
and Jonathon A. Cooper

LEXINGTON BOOKS
Lanham • Boulder • New York • London

Published by Lexington Books
An imprint of The Rowman & Littlefield Publishing Group, Inc.
4501 Forbes Boulevard, Suite 200, Lanham, Maryland 20706
www.rowman.com

6 Tinworth Street, London SE11 5AL, United Kingdom

British Library Cataloguing in Publication Information Available

Library of Congress Cataloging-in-Publication Data

Names: Jachimowski, Kayla G., author. | Cooper, Jonathon A., 1982- author.
Title: Police response to mental health calls for service : gatekeepers and street corner
    psychiatrists / Kayla G. Jachimowski and Jonathon A. Cooper.
Description: Lanham : Lexington Books, [2020] | Includes bibliographical references
    and index. | Summary: "This book explores the impact that training has on officer
    decision-making during calls for service where an individual has a mental health
    disorder, from both an empirical and historical perspective"—Provided by publisher.
Identifiers: LCCN 2020033152 (print) | LCCN 2020033153 (ebook) |
    ISBN 9781793601728 (cloth) | ISBN 9781793601742 (paperback) |
    ISBN 9781793601735 (epub)
Subjects: LCSH: Police services for the mentally ill. | Police training. | Mentally ill
    offenders.
Classification: LCC HV8079.3 .J33 2020 (print) | LCC HV8079.3 (ebook) |
    DDC 363.2/30874—dc23
LC record available at https://lccn.loc.gov/2020033152
LC ebook record available at https://lccn.loc.gov/2020033153

The authors dedicate this volume to the following individuals:

In loving memory of
Eunice I. Hurd
Thank you for your love, support, and being a great role model for me
to emulate for your great, great granddaughter. You are so very loved.
–KGJ

Lorenzo Groutage
–JC

Contents

Introduction

Picture this: an older male enters a veterinary clinic with a very dead cat. He proceeds to explain that he knows the cat is alive and he needs someone to save it. The veterinary technician responds, knowing the cat was euthanized in that clinic two days before, that they will get the doctor to check. With the stethoscope pressed against the cat's abdomen, the doctor apologizes but indicates there is no heartbeat. Agitated and upset, the gentleman tells the clinic they are responsible for killing his cat. After words are exchanged and the man leaves, the staff calls the police to let them know threats were made against the clinic. Upon learning the client's name, the officer tells the clinic that he knows this individual; he (the man) has "significant mental health problems" and he will personally tell him not to return to the clinic. The employees in the clinic look up past arrest records and determine they are in grave danger due to his past offenses and psychological history; despite his current behavior, research would on violence and mental health indicates he was unlikely to be a threat. This story is the motivation for writing this book and subsequent research on mental health and policing. It is our hope to continue reducing the stigma surrounding individuals with mental health disorders (MHDs).

To this end, our book's primary focus is examining one question which pertains to the diversion of individuals with a MHD away from the criminal justice system, and into more appropriate resources: (1) How does mental health training affect the way in which officers respond to mental health calls for service? Consideration is given to two other questions due to the interconnectedness of systems to the criminal justice system: (2) Does the officer's response to the call for service change based on professional or even personal relationships with mental health service providers? (3) Does police response change based on the number and type of mental health resources in the immediate area?

1

Ultimately, mental health is not just a policing issue; instead, it should be seen as a comprehensive problem that spans the criminal justice and mental health systems, to include medical and social service concerns (Cordner, 2006). Unfortunately, due to a number of societal and political shifts during the mid-twentieth century, persons with mental illness (PwMI) have become a "policing problem." In addition, traditional policing tactics have been shown to be ineffective, and sometimes dangerous for individuals with a MHD (Cordner, 2006). Thus, the focus needs to be on finding a solution to the influx of PwMI in the criminal justice system.

Our book is divided into two parts. Part I, "Policing and Mental Health Calls for Service," lays the groundwork for the second half of the book by introducing readers to how mental health has been understood historically in the United States; and what all of this has meant for policing. It is comprised of three chapters. Chapter 1, "An Introduction to the Problem," lays the foundation of what researchers understand, agree on, and where research has fallen short. This chapter is critical in carrying concepts throughout the rest of the book. Chapter 2, "Understanding Mental Health: A Brief History of American Practice," considers three interrelated topics: how is *mental health* defined and measured; the institutionalization of PwMI in the United States and the subsequent *de*institutionalization of the PwMI; and the impact that this would have on the American criminal justice system. Chapter 3, "Mental Health's Implications for Policing," extends the conversation from the preceding chapter explicitly into the realm of policing. It therefore considers the criminalization of mental health and its consequences for police officers and police agencies. It concludes with a theoretical framework to understand these relationships, preparatory for the second half of the book.

In the second part of our book, "State of Policing and Mental Health Calls for Service," we turn to the current trends of how police approach mental health calls for service. This section therefore considers two particular training milieus familiar to all police: the academy and in-service. The focus is on training and how it affects the potential actions of police, both at the start of their careers and in the middle of them. Chapter 4, "Police Training: General Patterns Related to CIT," considers how police are trained and hints at how this training may affect their behavior. Chapter 5, "Police Training: A More Detailed Look," scrutinizes the patterns discussed in chapter 4 with more detailed analyses and data. We pay special attention to crisis intervention teams (CIT), as well as consider, again, relevant empirical data.

We conclude with chapter 6, "Moving Forward: Theory and Practice." In this chapter, we proffer specific comments on theory and practice. In addition, we provide potential avenues for future research, in terms of research questions, methodological approaches, and novel ways to statistically assess the relationship between police, mental health training, and responding to mental health calls for service.

It is our intention to speak to the broader topic of the deinstitutionalization and criminalization of PwMI and its ramifications for police behavior. Specifically, in the last thirty years, criminal justice policy changes have continued to exacerbate the relationship between those with mental illness and the criminal justice system. Crackdowns on crimes that target quality-of-life concerns and substance use/abuse have created more opportunities for police interactions with PwMI (Thompson, Reuland, & Souweine, 2003). Moreover, Schulenberg (2015) argues police decision-making practices have complicated this relationship and added to the criminalization of mental illness. It is our hope that this volume will serve as a catalyst for change across all of these domains.

Part I

POLICING AND MENTAL HEALTH CALLS FOR SERVICE

Part I of our volume lays the groundwork for the second half of the book by introducing readers to the history of mental health in the United States as it applies to the criminal justice system. To this end, we spend considerable time on both the institutionalization of mental illness in the first half of the twentieth century and the subsequent deinstitutionalization of mental illness in the latter half of the twentieth century. We then consider what this means exactly for the police and provide some potential theoretical avenues for understanding how police can approach mental health calls for service.

Chapter 1

An Introduction to the Problem

WHAT DO WE KNOW AND WHAT DO WE NEED TO KNOW

As a society we are quick to label those with mental health disorders (MHDs) in the opening line of their illness: see *mental* illness. The idea is that somehow a psychological disorder is starkly different to a physical disorder or disease. Consider how many times a person has received flowers, cards, or balloons to "get well soon" after surgery; now consider how many times those same items are sent to an inpatient psychiatric facility. Society largely ignores the needs of those with MHDs (WHO, 2011); if society is not willing to recognize the problem, they are less likely to fight for funding and resources. To that point, consider Lucy Jo Matthews' (2016) story below:

> As I leant forward to blow out the candles on my cake, I took an extra deep breath realizing that this marked the point where I would have spent more of my life suffering from serious illness than I had not. It was my 30th birthday. I currently hold the dual diagnosis of having an Autistic Spectrum Disorder and Rapid Cycling Bipolar Disorder. (Matthew, 2016, p. 21)

> In my early days in the late 90s/early 00's the service [provided by the Community Mental Health Team (CMHT)] was largely coordinated by a small number of administrative staff who knew your name and had the time to engage with you and support your visit to the team. You knew them, and they knew you. When I returned [six years later] this had all changed—harassed and stressed staff (usually a different face each appointment) greeted you rudely while carrying out other tasks. There was no consistency, no oversight on contra-indicated

medication, and worse no beds unless you were critically ill. (Matthews, 2016, p. 26)

Her story is just one, among thousands, where there is a clear break-down between the mental health system and those who need treatment, unfortunately.

Yet, there remains a lack of cohesive agreement among researchers regarding the state of mental illness in the United States. To wit: society and researchers alike currently cannot agree on something as simple as whether there *is* such a thing as a mental illness (Bergner & Bunford, 2017; Varelius, 2009). For example, Varelius (2009) wistfully describes a situation in the mental health care community where individuals agree with physiological deficits but believe mental illnesses are fictitious conditions. At the other extreme, some scholars feel *any* violation of societal norms is a mental ill-ness (Bolton, 2008; Scheff, 1966). In the same vein, policing scholars report varying degrees of effectiveness in strategies designed explicitly to work with individuals with MHDs. These strategies can include anything from training police officers and cadets to appropriately interact with mentally disordered individuals to addressing the general perceptions among the police regard-ing those with mental health difficulties (Lord & Bjerregaard, 2014; Taheri, 2014; Watson, Morabito, Draine, & Ottati, 2008). At the end of the day, police have become not just gatekeepers to the criminal justice system for persons with mental illness (PwMI), but to adjust a famous phrase from Muir (1977), they have become street corner psychiatrists.

According to Lord and Bjerregaard (2014), the estimated rate of police interactions with individuals with a MHD is approximately 7–10 percent. This seems like a relatively small number of interactions when compared to the 90–93 percent of interactions which do not involve an individual with a MHD. *More so*, mental health research indicates dramatic spikes in the number of individuals in the community following deinstitutionalization (Harcourt, 2011; Kim, 2014; Lord & Bjerregaard, 2014), which would sug-gest a more *frequent* number of occurrences of interactions between officers and an individual with a MHD. The infrequency of police interaction with individuals with MHDs appears even more significant when one considers that the police are first responders, a point we consider in more depth through-out this volume. Simply, police are called *a lot*, for a number of reasons, so few of which (less than 10 percent) involved an individual with a MHD, it is easy to overlook the importance of this topic.

However, to put this in perspective, according to the Bureau of Justice Statistics (Banks, Handrix, Hickman, & Kyckelhahn, 2016) there are approx-imately 18,000 federal, state, and local policing agencies in the United States. These departments can range anywhere from a single officer to departments which are responsible for employing more than 30,000 officers and have jurisdiction in essentially every square inch of the United States. Given the innumerable number of interactions which occur every day between police and the public—from asking for directions to felony arrests—the 7–10 percent of interactions between police and an individual with a MHD arguably becomes an alarmingly high number. Just as a quick example, the BJS (2018) estimates there are approximately 253,587,400 people over the age of sixteen living in the United States. During the survey period, individuals were asked about their police interactions in the last twelve months. Estimates reveal 21.1 percent of people interaction with police officers in one year (Davis, Whyde, & Langston, 2018). Using these numbers (Davis, Whyde, & Langston, 2018), the numbers from Lord and Bjerregaard (2014) regarding PwMI interactions, and accounting *only* for police-initiated contact and resident-initiated contact, we estimate between 805,279 and 1,150,399 interactions between police officers and individuals with MHDs per year; or, 2,206–3,151 per day.

This high rate of interactions between the police and individuals with MHDs is driven by three interrelated phenomena: deinstitutionalization, the criminalization of the PwMI, and the very nature of the police as first responders. Deinstitutionalization refers to the emptying of state mental hospitals and facilities over time due to overcrowding, deterioration of the hospitals, and new medications that helped patients function without needing to be institutionalized (Torrey, Kennard, Eslinger, Lamb, & Pavle, 2010). In addition to political budgets that reduced or eliminated monies otherwise appropriated for state mental health facilities, there was a societal shift creating a pathway for more understanding of those with MHDs, albeit only slightly more open to the concept. Many of these changes were the result of political ideology independent of sound clinical practice. The reintegration of these patients into the community was never fully executed, insofar as individuals with mental illness often are subjected to arrest and prosecution in the criminal justice system for minor offenses due in part *to* their mental illness (Perez, Leifman, & Estrada, 2003).

Criminal punishment for minor offenses more likely to be caused by an individual with a MHD is referred to as the criminalization of mental illness. Consequently, the rate at which the PwMI are arrested, jailed, and otherwise enter the criminal justice system has labeled many such individuals as criminal. Subsequently, the PwMI in America have become part of the so-called revolving door of justice, characterized by frequent arrests for minor offenses, a long rap sheet, and minimal help to remove them from this pattern. The American criminal justice was never set up to work with an individual with a MHD, and despite its efforts to do so, it has consistently failed in this respect.

Deinstitutionalization and the criminalization of PwMI have had direct ramifications for the police. Because the police often are called to deal with not only crime but disorder, they interact disproportionately with PwMI. Therefore, police officers act as gatekeepers for the criminal justice system for individuals with mental health problems (Jennings & Hudak, 2005; Lord & Bjerregaard, 2014). Some researchers provide catchier names, such as "street-corner psychiatrists" or "social workers." Whatever title one may want to apply, police are primarily law enforcers and order maintainers, not psychologists. It remains true that as long as members of society place calls for service related to an individual with a MHD *to the police*, PwMI will continue to lack appropriate resources to manage their disorders. Ultimately, whatever disagreement may exist between the mental health community and the criminal justice system in terms of how best to work with an individual with a MHD, given both deinstitutionalization and the criminalization of PwMI, police officers will continue to be responsible for the intersection of mental health, crime, justice, and order (Steadman, Deane, Borum, & Morrissey, 2000).

As we have noted, PwMI represent an estimated 7–10 percent of all police contact. According to Akins, Burkhardt, Lanfear, Amorim, and Stevens (2014), individuals with serious mental illness (SMI) make up, at most, 5 percent of the population. Not only is there a disproportionate amount of contact between the police and PwMI, but PwMI generally have repeated contact with police. Nearly half of PwMI have had a repeat occurrence with police within sixty days of their initial interaction (Akins, Burkhardt, Lanfear, Amorim, & Stevens, 2014). Unfortunately, police departments often lack the training, policies, and procedures to adequately manage the responsibility of being a gatekeeper for the PwMI (Ruiz & Miller, 2004). For example, police typically are wary of individuals with mental illness because they are perceived as being extra-dangerous and unpredictable (Ruiz & Miller, 2004). This is reinforced, not only in part, by society's negative views of those with mental illnesses, but also in part by how the police are trained to deal with *any* situation. Police are trained to immediately take control of a situation and retain control with the express purpose of protecting their person, the public, including any victim or victims, and the suspect(s). Such perceptions and training force upon the police two emotional stimuli: compassionately recognizing the need for treatment and judiciously arresting a person to protect the community (Jennings & Hudak, 2005). Such mixed stimuli about how to respond to an individual with a MHD can prevent an officer from seeing past safety concerns to mental health needs, because, as a general rule, safety trumps other concerns for the police. Historically, this focus on control and safety has led to violence between police and an individual with a MHD (Morabito et al., 2010).

Indeed, a call for service that involves an individual with a MHD can be, at best, untenable for the police.

While the burden is on police officers, the responsibility rests on the mental health system. Consider that even as officers and their departments are requesting and receiving training in de-escalation strategies (including such topics as being able to identify a person with MHD), the lack of resources in the mental health care field makes it exceedingly difficult for police (Lord & Bjerregaard, 2014). A more recent solution to this problem is crisis intervention teams (CIT), which were developed to decrease the number of violent encounters between individuals with MHDs and the police (Morabito et al., 2010) through specialized training (Taheri, 2014). In general, CIT involves training police officers to act as a liaison between the first responders and the mental health system (Compton, Broussard, Reed, Crisafio, & Watson, 2015). Training for these teams includes information on mental health, local resources, and the law (Taheri, 2014). However, to date, the research remains inconsistent on the effectiveness of CIT in reducing the use of force and violent encounters with individuals with MHD (Morabito et al., 2012). Mobile crisis teams and community crisis specialists have also been explored as possibilities to decrease the rate at which individuals with MHD are placed in the criminal justice system. However, they are not as popular as CIT and suffer from even fewer empirically and methodologically rigorous studies (Kisely et al., 2010; Lee et al., 2015; Lord & Bjerregaard, 2014; Rosenbaum, 2010). To make matters muddier, the mental health care field has yet to conclusively agree on definitions which are critical to the advancement of policies and strategies to divert individuals from the criminal justice system (Begner & Bunford, 2017). For example, the failed attempt to define core aspects of MHDs using empirical support instead of conceptual or normative definitions (Bergner & Bunford, 2017). As laws remain unchanged, policies left outdated, and empirical evidence lacking cohesiveness, it becomes difficult, if not unfair, to expect police officers to adapt their responses to what we are calling *mental health calls for service* (MHCFS). We use the term *MHCFS* to denote those calls for service wherein the primary suspect, or at least the person to whom the majority of the police officer's attention is directed, is an individual with a MHD.

Additionally, the lack of theoretical support as a pillar of policy implication research regarding the interactions between police and individual with MHD is another deficit of this research area. Thus, it is important to consider applicable theories to inform our research. Although this volume's purpose is not theory testing, there are three theoretical frameworks that will not only inform our discussion, but that we hope to harness to better direct discussions on interactions between the police and individuals with MHD. These theories speak to the importance of police training on mental health, clearer procedures for MHCFS, and the likelihood of police diverting individuals with mental illness from the criminal justice system. The three theories we find most applicable and useful for exploring MHCFS are as follows:

- *Peplau's Theory of Interpersonal Relations*, which examines the relationships between nurses and their clients seen in a clinical setting; however, for our purposes, the *interpersonal relations* concepts are appropriated and discussed in light of police and an individual with a MHD interactions (Peplau, 1997). More specifically, creating a skill where officers can use core values to create interpersonal experiences when responding to MHCFS. Peplau's theory, though generalizable to general nurse practitioners, is most effective in psychiatric nursing. With concepts like increasing communication among a population of people who have a difficult time communicating and relatedness, there is a clear relevance offering guidance from officers who are responding to MHCFS.
- *Structural Holes* and *Weak Ties* are compared and contrasted to highlight the importance of expanding a social network away from one centralized location, such as a police department, to include several mental health resources that can provide critical information and services to police officers. These theoretical concepts are drawn directly from Burt (1992) and Granovetter (1973). Though competing theories at the time, the application to policing is more or less the same; the more individuals an officer knows from outside their department, the more they will learn about resources, experiences, and approaches to policing individuals with MHDs.
- Finally, *Systems Theory* is used to examine the importance of changes in systematic organizational behaviors, the effect that behavioral change has on other systems, and the ways in which this relates to the poor relationship between the mental health and criminal justice systems (Morgan, 1998; Stewart & Ayres, 2001). This theory is especially appropriate when discussing the police as it has been the dominant theory directing the form of the American criminal justice system—including the police—since the 1960s (cf. Klofas, Hippe, & Maguire, 2010 for a detailed review of this process).

Overall, the research about MHCFS is not rich, but the studies which exist suggest that most MHCFS are handled informally by the police (Engel & Silver, 2001). Typically, officers have broad discretion over how they resolve calls involving individuals with MHDs, which often are minor in nature (Reuland, Schwarzfeld, & Draper, 2009). As Reuland, Schwarzfeld, and Draper (2009) point out, such informality can be missed opportunities to refer individuals to effective treatment interventions. Understanding how and why police respond to MHCFS will therefore fill an important gap in the policing and mental health literature.

Chapter 2

Understanding Mental Health

A Brief History of American Practice

To summarize the mental health practice in the United States would be to write nothing short of inconclusive, frequently misled (despite good intentions, mostly), and consistently behind the times. As we alluded to in the previous chapter, mental health care providers, advocates, and researchers, to say nothing of lawmakers and those who administer the laws, disagree on what is meant by the term "mental health," let alone the implications of mental health for behavior. To better understand these issues, and why they are important, there is arguably no better place to start than with American advocate Dorothea Dix, who was vital to reforming mental health during the last half of the nineteenth century.

Better known as Dorothy, Ms. Dix's interest in mental health was sparked after witnessing the treatment of mentally disordered prison inmates in her role as a Sunday school teacher. During her weekly visit to the local jail, Ms. Dix has been reported to describe the plight of her experience as disturbing: "[i]nsane persons confined within this [Massachusetts] Commonwealth, in cages, stalls, pens! Chained, naked beaten with rods, and lashed into obedience" (Tiffany, 1890, p. 76). Soon thereafter, Ms. Dix started a campaign which would eventually culminate in the allocation of state-directed monies for asylums to house individuals with serious mental illness (SMI) in the United States (Schutt & Goldfinger, 2011).

This set off a domino effect of states' laws regarding the treatment of the mentally ill across the United States. Such laws were typically titled "State Care Acts." For example, The New York State Care Act of 1890 both standardized and centralized the financial responsibility of caring for individuals with mental illness to the state (Goldman & Grob, 2006). This had a number of unintended consequences, however, such as increasing the number of elderly individuals placed in state mental hospitals (cf. Goldman & Grob,

13

2006). There is a general sense, then, that state sponsoring of institutions for the mentally ill served to increase the number of individuals with MHD who were committed, at least at a nominal level. Not all researchers agree with this assessment, however. To wit, McNally (2012) suggests relatively few individuals (in the early 1900s) would have been recognized or diagnosed as clinically depressed or anxious compared to today. Simply, this was during a time when you could be committed to a mental health institution for preferring fictional stories over nonfiction (novel reading) but overlooked as sad opposed to depressed.

Nevertheless, in the 1950s, when the number of those with MHD housed in state institutions was at its peak, state mental health facilities began seeing societal, economic, and political shifts *away from* the interest and demand for adequate care for individuals with a mental health diagnosis (Harcourt, 2011). This presaged the deinstitutionalization which would have its heyday in the late 1970s and early 1980s. At the time, such efforts as The Joint Commission on Mental Illness and Health created in 1955, The National Institute of Mental Health's (NIMH) programs, and the Community Mental Health Centers Act of 1963 (Goldman & Grob, 2006; Harcourt, 2011; Kim, 2014) began the societal rebuff from state-sponsored mental health.

Even from as brief a historical survey as the above two paragraphs provide, it is rather clear that defining mental illness is a complicated task for researchers and practitioners alike; if for no other reason than the definition *shifts* based on cultural, political, economic, and scientific factors (Goldman & Grob, 2006; Granello & Granello, 2000). To further obfuscate matters, the fields of neurobiology and psychology have both provided their two cents worth concerning what *is* and *is not* a mental illness (McNally, 2012). How a person defines "mental health" (and consequently mental illness or disorder) may be narrow, such as SMI, or broader to include nonserious mental illness (nSMI) (Goldman & Grob, 2006). The issue is not one of semantics, however, as it has considerable real-world implications.

Increasingly, mental health practitioners and researchers (to say nothing of laypersons) tend to erroneously treat such words as *psychopathology*, *mental illness*, *abnormality*, and *mental disorder* almost synonymously (Bergner & Bunford, 2017). This may be, partially, due to what Bergner and Bunford (2017) explain as the attempt "to settle this question of the meaning of the concept 'mental disorder,' not on the basis of empirical evidence, but from our armchairs" (p. 26). This is corroborated in part by Granello and Granello (2000), who point out that even the *Diagnostic and Statistical Manual of Mental Disorders* (*DSM*, then in its fourth official iteration), the most commonly used and most comprehensive collection of mental health diagnoses, fails to offer full definitions of psychiatric disorders.

Speaking specifically about the deficiency in uniformity of defining mental illness among researchers, Varelius (2009) enumerates a multitude of different definitions employed throughout the literature. For example, Fulford (1989, as cited in Varelius, 2009) defined mental disorder as an individual's incapacity to engage in their environment without a breakdown, whereas Gert and Culver (2004, cited in Varelius, 2009) defined mental disorder as a clinically significant behavioral or psychological pattern, or display of symptoms which occur simultaneously to distress and disability with the potential to lead to death, pain, or the loss of freedom. Lastly, although certainly not a comprehensive overview of how researchers have historically defined mental illness and mental health, Wakefield (1992) argued that there is a lack of conclusiveness on the definition of mental illness *because* there are varying definitions of the individual terms composing the phrase "mental illness disorder." Thus, the words *mental, illness,* and *disorder* all vary in how they are defined between different people and according to different contexts. The problem in defining "mental illness disorder" is therefore not only compounded, but exponentially so. Varelius (2009) goes so far as to argue that the words within the *definitions* of mental disorder are themselves difficult to track down, further complicating the matter.

Consider the newly updated DSM (in its fifth iteration as of 2015) and compare its definition of mental illness to that provided by the U.S. Surgeon General. First, the DSM-V defines mental illness as:

A mental disorder is a syndrome characterized by clinically significant disturbance in an individual's cognition, emotion regulation, or behavior that reflects a dysfunction in the psychological, biological, or developmental processes underlying mental functioning. Mental disorders are usually associated with significant distress or disability in social, occupational, or other important activities. An expectable or culturally approved response to a common stressor or loss, such as the death of a loved one, is not a mental disorder. Socially deviant behavior (e.g., political, religious, or sexual) and conflicts that are primarily between the individual and society are not mental disorders unless the deviance or conflict results from a dysfunction in the individual, as described above. (American Psychiatric Association, 2000)

In contrast, the U.S. Surgeon General stated:

Mental health is a state of successful performance of mental function, resulting in productive activities, fulfilling relationships with other people, and an ability to adapt to change and to cope with adversity. . . . Mental illness is the term that refers collectively to all diagnosable mental disorders. Mental disorders are health conditions that are characterized by alterations in thinking, mood, or behavior (or some combination thereof) associated with distress and/or impaired functioning. (pp. 4–5, as cited in Goldman & Grob, 2006)

The issue is not that they are mutually exclusive; it is that they are not in agreement. Much like the Gospel narratives of the Christian scriptures, they tend to emphasize different aspects or even contradict one another in subtle and not-so-subtle ways. And, similar to the Gospel narratives, this ambiguity gives *carte blanche* to various interpretations, each with their own institutional implications. The fact of the matter is that mental health and illness are not like pornography *a la* the Supreme Court: one does not just know it when they see it. The full implication of these definitional struggles will be borne out throughout our book and revisited with special focus in the final chapter. First, though, we explore one of the most immediate and lasting implications of definitional disagreement in the realm of mental health: deinstitutionalization.

THE DEINSTITUTIONALIZATION
OF MENTAL ILLNESS

As noted above, state psychiatric hospital populations were at its highest in 1955, with over half a million inpatients. By 2003, however, this number dropped from 559,000 to approximately 47,000 (cf. Davis, Fulginiti, Kriegal, & Brekke, 2012). This decrease was the result of several cooccurring political decisions and changes in the social winds regarding attitudes toward mental illness. It would mark a turning point for PwMI both in terms of resources publicly available to them and in terms of how the state would approach the behavior of individuals with MHDs. Specifically: there is a direct connection between the deinstitutionalization of state-sponsored psychiatric hospitals and the criminalization of mental illness (Jones, 2015; Mechanic & Rochefort, 1990; Torrey et al., 2010), a connection that remains salient today, particularly for the police.

The term "psychiatric deinstitutionalization" has both a normative and practical meaning. Normatively, it refers to a philosophy of shifting the burden of mental health care from hospitals to community-based facilities that are largely privatized. Practically, it means the emptying and closing of state mental hospitals (Kim, 2014; Torrey et al., 2010). This shift is borne out by the numbers: by 1954, there were approximately 1,200 inpatient facilities and more than 1,400 outpatient facilities by 1959 (Accordino, Porter, & Morse, 2001).

One of the most important and substantial contributing factors to the societal shift toward community-based treatment for individuals with MHDs and, subsequently, deinstitutionalization was the *Community Mental Health Centers* (CMHC) *Act of 1963* (Mechanic & Rochefort, 1990), which grew out of the *Mental Health Study Act of 1955*. CMHC mandated state and local mental health facilities to increase the rate of treatment in community facilities as opposed to purely inpatient approaches (Lynum & Hill, 2015). This changing focus was evident in one of John F. Kennedy's messages to the United States Congress where he outlined a plan to move forward toward community health care by setting an actual numeric target: a 50 percent decrease in the number of patients in state hospitals and asylums within twenty years (Davis et al., 2012; Harcourt, 2011; Mechanic & Rochefort, 1990).

The CMHC succeeded in reducing the number of inpatients in psychiatric hospitals. In fact, deinstitutionalization ramped up so quickly that twelve years after its enactment the inpatient population had decreased by 59.3 percent; by 1975, that population was down by 62 percent (Harcourt, 2011; Mechanic & Rochefort, 1990); and within twenty-five years, the number of state hospital inpatients had decreased by 75 percent (Harcourt, 2011). Ultimately, the rate of inpatients at state-run mental asylums and hospitals would decrease by 90 percent (Davis et al., 2012).

As with almost everything in the United States after 1950—society, religion, politics, norms, *inter alia*—attitudes, science, and subsequently policy toward mental health began to change dramatically as a consequence of World War II (Accordino et al., 2001; Harcourt, 2011; Kim, 2014; Davis et al., 2012; Mechanic & Rochefort, 1990; Rochefort, 1984). Indeed, even prior to the end of World War II, mental health became an important issue because military personnel were being discharged due to failure to pass psychiatric tests. Such servicemen would be labeled "psychiatric casualties," and would eventually account for more than two million men who were discharged from the Army during World War II. The ultimate result of such psychiatric casualties of war was that mental health became a public issue that grew as something openly discussed despite being previously overlooked or dismissed. Consequently, mental health diagnoses rose. In response, states began training more mental health professionals to manage the large number of men who were suffering from a neuropsychiatric disorder. This development occurred in tandem with a desire to look for more community-based treatments and other alternatives to institutionalization (Davis et al., 2012; Mechanic & Rochefort, 1990).

A second important contributing factor leading to the deinstitutionalization of mental health facilities was a shift in priority from hospitalization and institutionalization to drug therapy, especially for SMI (cf. Davis et al., 2012; Kim, 2014; Mechanic & Rochefort, 1990; Rochefort, 1984). By 1956, over two million patients had been prescribed chlorpromazine (more commonly known by its brand name, Thorazine). Indeed, the majority of states were, by this time, prescribing some type of antipsychotic drug to their patients (Harcourt, 2011). In some respects, this development was a move away from the more torturous methods of treatment (no matter the intention) for individuals with MHDs. To that point, prior to this increased preference for drug treatment, the most common mode of "therapy" for individuals with MHDs were electroshock therapy and lobotomy (Harcourt, 2011). Antipsychotic drugs, such as chlorpromazine, quickly became readily available during the mid-1950s (Kim, 2014). The shift from institutionalization to community-based alternatives involving psychotherapeutic drugs was encouraged by research indicating that antipsychotic drugs were fully capable of "curing" a multitude of disparate diagnoses, from depression to schizophrenia (Kim, 2014; Rochefort, 1984). In any case, antipsychotic drugs reduced the need for physical restraints and other previously employed tranquilizers. This all added credence to both the need and the inevitability of reform for mental health services, both in terms of the institutions that administered such services and in terms of how society understood mental illness (Davis et al., 2012; Rochefort, 1984).

One consequence of both drug therapy and the military's interest in mental health was a series of assays by the military on different therapies. This led to major advances in therapeutic psychology (Rochefort, 1990) and the popularization of the field in psychiatry known as psychiatric epidemiology. The importance of this field of study's research on the understanding and quality of mental health services cannot be overstated (Rochefort, 1990; Davis et al., 2012). Psychiatric epidemiology was unique insofar as its practitioners found that proper treatment for PwMI must include not only their individual characteristics, but their socioeconomic and demographic backgrounds (Rochefort, 1990) also. As with the increased use of antipsychotic medicines, this did lead to an improvement in the overall treatment and understanding of those with mental health illnesses, in addition leading the public away from inpatient approaches to mental health services toward community-based approaches. Ultimately, this would prove to be both more humane and cost-effective and would serve to further change the public's opinion about mental health and its treatment.

This shift in public opinion was reinforced in 1965 with the passing of Medicaid and Medicare. Such legislation came with a greater awareness of the need and viability of mental healthcare reform and moved the United States further toward a public/private collaboration rather than a purely public approach. For example, both programs offered PwMI who did not have family support to be cared for in nursing homes by *dividing* the cost between the state and federal government (Gronfein, 1985); thus, a level of discretion in how such programs were to be funded. Even though states would pay no more than 50 percent of the cost to house an individual with a MHD in a nursing home (Mechanic & Rochefort, 1990), this was a major shift in budgetary priorities. During this period, we saw an expansion of such nursing homes as well as other social welfare programs, including Social Security Income (SSI) and Social Security Disability Insurance (SSDI), which also facilitated the reintegration of PwMI back into the community (Davis et al., 2012; Gronfein, 1985; Kim, 2014). Ultimately, Medicare and Medicaid would solidify the political and social move away from state-run mental hospitals as an "ideal" solution (Davis et al., 2012; Harcourt, 2011).

In the midst of these political, scientific, and social changes, the public and government were being made aware of the numerous allegations of the poor conditions in mental health care facilities. This only served to fuel the public's growing interest in such institutions and would result in even more demands for change—this time from civil liberties advocates (Davis et al., 2012; Harcourt, 2011; Kim, 2014; Rochefort, 1984). Such advocates focused their challenges on two specific legal policies: procedural due process and minimum standards of care. Up to this point, there had been minimal procedural standards for committing someone to a mental institution involuntarily. The justification for doing so, similar to readers familiar with the American juvenile justice system and falling under the same umbrella as *parens patriae*, was that the involuntary commitment was not punitive but was instead protective; to this end, it was not seen as a violation of civil liberties. Therefore, due process was not a requisite.

Two court opinions were crucial to challenging and changing this conceptualization of involuntary commitment: *Wyatt v. Stickney* (1972) and *O'Connor v. Donaldson* (1975). Together, these cases set the precedent that PwMI had the right to be treated *and* treated with a minimum standard of care. Further, it articulated the criteria for *minimum standard of care* that an individual has the right to receive (Prigmore & Davis, 1973; *Wyatt v. Stickney*, 1972). The rulings mandated that hospitals in the state of Alabama treat PwMI with a qualified mental health professional, teach patients life skills, instruct them in coping mechanisms that could be employed upon release to the community, provided for a right to privacy, *inter alia* (cf. Prigmore & Davis, 1973). In *O'Connor v. Donaldson* (1975), the U.S. Supreme Court went a step further and developed the dangerousness standard: that a PwMI could not be held against their will unless they were perceived as a danger to themselves and/ or others (cf. Fields, 1976). By removing the *ad hoc* nature of involuntary commitment, the courts effectively took away the single tool that made state hospitals necessary.

After the *Stickney* and *O'Connor* decisions, numerous state-run hospitals were unable to meet the newly mandated standard of care and were therefore forced to close. Concomitantly, the advent of effective antipsychotics, therapy, and the creation of Medicare and Medicaid, public perception about mental illness, PwMI, all created a rapid and substantial shift in attitudes about mental health treatment. This culminated in the almost complete deinstitutionalization of mental illness, shifting the burden from the government to local communities and families. The unintended and problematic consequences of this shift were manifold as some families and communities were simply unprepared and unequipped to pick up the torch. As a result, many PwMI were left to fend for themselves, often becoming homeless and criminal in the process (Jones, 2015; Lamb, 1984; Mechanic & Rochefort, 1990). In effect, deinstitutionalization created a society that demanded community-based treatments for individuals with mental illness without the means to adequately provide resources for all of these people (Lamb, 1984). The end result was a new population of individuals who suddenly became the responsibility of the American criminal justice system. The criminalization of mental illness has become an unforeseen consequence of deinstitutionalization (Ringhoff, Rapp, & Robst, 2012).

THE CRIMINALIZATION OF MENTAL ILLNESS

In tandem with deinstitutionalization, mental illness gradually became criminalized. Abramson, in 1972, was the first to use the term, *criminalization of mental illness*, and is generally attributed as coining it. This refers to placing someone in the criminal justice system, via arrest, whose behavior stems from a mental health problem and who should be transported to a psychiatric hospital. This recourse, handing responsibility over to the criminal justice system, ultimately led to a lack of funding and resources that would normally allow for psychiatric commitment or, at least, therapy (Fisher, Silver, & Wolff, 2006). The criminalization of mental illness grew out of the deinstitutionalization movement: even though deinstitutionalization promised to shift government funds from state psychiatric hospitals to the community to support the *new* community-based treatment programs for individuals with MHDs (Chaimowitz, 2011), this was never realized. Rather, far less money was invested in the community. The result was that numerous individuals with MHDs ended up in the criminal justice system instead of psychiatric hospitals or any community-based treatment facilities. Criminalization was *not* a policy; it was the *de facto* result of deinstitutionalization.

Evidence for the criminalization of mental illness abound and are not difficult to find. For example, Perez and colleagues (2003) found that PwMIs are extremely likely to be subject to both arrest and prosecution for minor offenses for which most individuals would be ticketed or verbally warned. They also discovered that diversion strategies—including community support groups and even civil commitment—are rarely applied to PwMIs. Once an individual with MHD is part of the "revolving door of justice," it becomes increasingly difficult for them to end up anywhere *but* prison. Rather than receiving needed services, individuals with MHDs are placed behind bars where they merely can be "controlled." Two crimes in particular have been harnessed against individuals with MHDs in ways that can reasonably be labeled discriminatory: substance use and homelessness.

Substance Use and Mental Illness

In the 1990s, Carey and Correia (1998) suggested that PwMI whose diagnoses were severe were more likely to have comorbid substance use patterns compared to PwMI who were not diagnosed with severe mental health disorders. Contemporary literature indicates the rate of comorbidity has increased both with respect to alcohol and drug use since the late 1990s (Carey & Correia, 1998; Slate, Bluffington-Vollum, & Johnson, 2013). This is due, in part, to an increase in self-medicating practices among PwMIs (Robinson, Sareen, Cox, & Bolton, 2009; Slate, Buffington-Vollum, & Johnson, 2013; Thornton et al., 2012). Self-medicating practices increased in response to deinstitutionalization: as community-based mental health facilities grew without promised funding, acquiring needed medication became both more expensive and more difficult. Consequently, PwMIs found other ways—both licit and illicit, but certainly not therapeutic—to cope with their mental illnesses (Moore & Elkavich, 2008; Slate et al., 2013). Substances (alcohol and drugs) are often employed by PwMI as a form of self-medication for other reasons, as well. As Slate and colleagues (2013) reported (and as corroborated by Thornton et al., 2012), illicit drugs/alcohol use not only provides PwMI with a sense of normalcy but also provides a pleasurable experience. This is in contradistinction to psychiatric medications whose side effects can be less than pleasurable. Unfortunately, the literature also suggests that PwMI who are diagnosed with SMIs *and* substance abuse disorders are more likely to exhibit extremely negative behavior, including criminal and violent (Gonzalez et al., 2007; Slate et al., 2013; Swartz et al., 1998).

Homelessness and Mental Illness

Since deinstitutionalization did not deliver on its promise for community-based treatment centers, many PwMI without families or monetary means found themselves on the streets, homeless, and eventually incarcerated. This remains true today. On average, there are approximately 636,017 individuals who are homeless every day; of that, 25 to 35 percent suffer not just from a mental illness, but from a SMI as well (Davis et al., 2012). Although the causal link between mental health and homelessness is not yet empirically

understood (homelessness is considered an "intermediate factor" when discussing the pathway to incarceration, cf. White, Chafetz, Collins-Bride, &
Nickens, 2006), scholars are agreed that there is a relationship between deinstitutionalization and homelessness (Lamb, 1984), if for no other reason than
prior to deinstitutionalization, PwMI *did* have somewhere to live: state psychiatric hospitals. As Lamb (1984) has argued, without the rapid divestment
of individuals from state-run hospitals, homelessness of PwMIs would not
have occurred in such staggering numbers and in quite the small-time frame.
Further, Perez, Leifman, and Estrada (2003) point out that when individuals
with MHDs do not receive adequate treatment, and are left without appropriate resources, the likelihood of their homelessness is almost inevitable, and
their entrance into the criminal justice system becomes almost as a matter
of course. Gur (2010) and Perez and colleagues (2003) each argue that even
though criminologists seem to downplay the impact mental health has on
being arrested, research consistently shows the police are more likely to arrest
individuals with a mental illness for minor offenses than individuals without
a mental health diagnosis—including homelessness. It is to the subject of the
criminal justice system and PwMIs that we now turn.

MENTAL ILLNESS AND THE
CRIMINAL JUSTICE SYSTEM

Although our volume focuses on the relationship between the police and
those with MHDs, it is important (and necessary) to remember that all parts
of the justice system are intimately connected. These connections are not just
legal; they also affect the discretion of police officers. This consideration is
twofold: First, the outcomes of policies and laws affected the officers who
respond, the court system which tries the case, and the correctional system.
It cannot be overlooked that any change in the functionality of police should
also dictate a change in the other subsystems of the criminal justice system.
Second, there are extralegal factors which directly account for part of an
officer's use of discretion at the scene (this is explored further in chapters
4 and 5). This is as true for how police approach PwMI as it is for all other
such encounters. It becomes even more important to recognize that, generally speaking, PwMI are far more likely to be disproportionately represented
during *all* stages of the American criminal justice system (Vogel, Stephens,
& Siebels, 2014).

At numerous points in the process, the justice system can divert PwMI
away from the criminal justice system and into what might be termed a
"mental health system." Indeed, one consequence of deinstitutionalization
has been the creation of two disjointed systems—one for mental health and

one for criminal justice—which created a dangerous situation where both systems functioned, more or less, independently (cf. Torrey et al., 2010; Vogel, Stephens, & Siebels, 2014). In so many cases, the discretion to divert a PwMI *away* from the justice system or to keep them in the criminal justice system is not made by a clinician, but rather by a criminal justice actor, including the police (Montross, 2016), who have traditionally held the role of gatekeepers to the justice system. In effect, as a result of deinstitutionalization and the greater role that police now play in the lives of many PwMI, police have also become gatekeepers to the mental health system: a system to which they do not belong.

Prior to fully considering this relationship between police and those with mental illness, we briefly explore the roles of the courts and correctional facilities vis-à-vis individuals with a MHD. To have this discussion, we feel it is important to note this section does not flow in a chronological order, but instead focus on important, fundamental, practices of processing individuals with MHDs through the criminal justice system. We recognize, both chronologically, and given the general criminal justice process (police courts corrections) that the policing discipline was making changes to policy before mental health courts and changes to the correctional system occurred.

Mental Health Courts

Given the overrepresentation of PwMI in the legal system, coupled with their frequent failure in the traditional adversarial model of law, brought about the recognition for an alternative court system for individuals with MHDs. Thus, this general trend in the United States toward alternative courts encompassed the needs of individuals with MHDs through the so-called Mental Health Courts (MHC). According to researchers (e.g., Vogel, Stephens, & Siebels, 2014), MHCFS have been repeatedly demonstrated to be an effective diversion for PwMI's away from the justice system and into the mental health system. These courts are most effective in matching an individual with a MHD with community resources upon reentry that match their diagnostic needs. MCHs are an example of "problem-solving courts," sometimes called specialty courts: Such courts are open to specific populations or offenses (cf. Castellano & Anderson, 2013). The most common problem-solving court in the United States is for drug and alcohol offenses, and it is on their framework that MHCFS were first created in 1997. By 2009, there were more than 250 MHCFS across the nation; this number continues to increase nationwide (Almquist & Dodd, 2009; Castellano & Anderson, 2013).

The three goals of any MHC are the following: (1) provide clinical approaches to reducing recidivism; (2) effectively decriminalize mental illness; and (3) provide a more therapeutic restructuring of the criminal justice process (Almquist & Dodd, 2009; Castellano & Anderson, 2013). In order for an individual to be diverted into a MHC, they must meet specific criteria (unfortunately, there are as of yet no standardized criteria across MHCFS). Generally speaking, all MHCFS employ some variation of case management process, which can include social workers, treatment service professionals, probation officers, judges, and other courtroom actors (Ray, 2014). After a treatment plan is developed, the defendant is monitored closely to ensure the guidelines are followed; such treatment plans can include regular therapy sessions and participation in drug screening, among other things (Almquist & Dodd, 2009; Ray, 2014). The approach is best understood as being *collaborative* rather than *adversarial* (Almquist & Dodd, 2009; Castellano & Anderson, 2013; Hiday & Ray, 2010; McNeil & Binder, 2007; Ray, 2014).

Despite the empirical support for MHCFS mentioned above, there remains a difference of opinion on their effectiveness to actually reduce recidivism for participants (Almquist & Dodd, 2009; Castellano & Anderson, 2013; Vogel, Stephens, & Siebels, 2014). For example, even though Ray (2014) points out that the majority of research finds that most individuals have lower rates of recidivism after completing their treatment plan than before entering the MHC, other studies show no change to recidivism when compared with PwMI who follow the traditional criminal justice court process (Ray, 2014; Hiday & Ray, 2010). What is more, there are criticisms that, along with no standardized criteria for admission to a MHC, such courts are simply not inclusive enough. For example, most of the individuals who go through MHCFS must be nonviolent offenders, and more specifically, only have committed misdemeanors (Vogel, Stephens, & Siebels, 2014).

Though, admittedly, the corpus of research on MHC and recidivism reduction suffer from the same methodological limitations as do pretty much every social scientific study. Vogel, Stephens, and Siebels (2014) note multiple reasons why such criticisms exist regarding MHCFS. There are few studies that employ comparison groups, almost none which use control groups, and almost all studies employ cross-sectional designs with limited or zero follow-ups. More specifically, studies which have been done have small sample size based solely on one jurisdiction at a time. Given the "survival" nature of recidivism, it is particularly problematic that there are almost no longitudinal studies (Hiday & Ray, 2010). It is safest, perhaps, to say that while MHCFS remain a promising approach to working with a justice system involved PwMI, the promise itself remains somewhat unchecked.

Mentally Ill Individuals in Prison

While our focus in this book is on the police and their interactions with PwMIs, perhaps no other institution associated with the administration of justice has felt the impact of deinstitutionalization quite like the corrections system in America. To wit: some studies report more than half of inmates, in both jails and prisons, suffer from some form of mental illness according to James and Glaze (2006); whereas, just seven years prior, the BJS reported only 16.3 percent of jail inmates had a mental health disorder. And, with regard to SMI, Steadman, Osher, Robbing, Case, and Samuels (2009) reported just under 17 percent had symptoms of SMI.

While some disagree with the methodology used in the James and Glaze (2006) report, and others argue Steadman et al. (2009) only reviewed two states worth of data, we present equally uneven results to highlight our point of inconsistency. Prins (2014) conducted a systematic review of mental illness in U.S. state prisons. His review included twenty-eight total articles between 1989 and 2013. The numbers based on a broad set of categories regarding mental health range from 10 percent significant psychiatric disability (Dvoskin & Steadman, 1989) to 62 percent having major depression (Staton et al., 2003) (as cited in Prin, 2014). More specific to SMI, for example, rates for schizophrenia among the prison population were as low as 1.2 percent (Baillargeon et al., 2000) to as high as 6.4 percent (DiCataldo et al., 1995) (as cited in Prin, 2014). Finally, more recent studies have reported the prevalence of individuals with MHDs in prison ranging from 20 percent (any combination of mental illness) (Jachimowski, 2018b) to 37 percent (told by a mental health practitioner that they had a mental illness) (Bronson & Berzofsky, 2017); though both report that major depressive disorder accounted for the largest portion of mental illness. The conclusion of this lengthy but not exhaustive list of studies, despite the disagreement, is there are far more individuals with MHDs in prison than there should be. Given that the "prime directive" of correctional facilities is safe custody, at the cost of therapy and treatment, it is not surprising that inmates with MHDs face a scarcity of resources and programmatic options (Adams & Ferrandino, 2008).

To be clear, the criminal justice system was not envisioned, designed, or implemented to function in a way which would provide significant mental health treatment. In fact, the current state of the criminal justice system is ill-equipped to handle the influx of individuals with MHDs that continues to increase since deinstitutionalization. Thus, we are left with correctional institutions being forced to become "pseudo-mental health" facilities. Despite attempts to find and use effective treatment, the majority of individuals who need mental health treatment do not receive it during their incarceration (Vogel, Stephens, & Siebels, 2014). This poses a number of concerns: individuals with MHDs are more likely to commit frequent (minor) infractions, have an increased rate of victimization when compared to individuals without MHDs, and violence or misunderstandings on the part of correctional officers (COs) due to a lack of training.

First, PwMIs are more likely to commit prison infractions, such as disobeying a rule, when compared to inmates who are not diagnosed with a MHD. Mental illness can often diminish one's ability to think rationally, which can lead to a variety of inappropriate behaviors, including: forms of unintentional aggression, opposition to general instruction, the inability to follow the rules, and low-level violence (e.g., pushing as opposed to attacking someone with an improvised weapon) (Benton & Masciadrelli, 2013; Geiman, 2007). The lack of training, on the part of the correctional staff, often leads to inappropriately handling inmates with MHDs when they commit such minor infractions. This can create a hostile environment for everyone—COs, PwMI, and other inmates (Adams & Ferrandino, 2008). It is too frequently the case that such inmates, unable to conform to prison norms and expectations, are remanded to solitary confinement rather than being offered a variety of treatment options (Adams & Ferrandino, 2008; Benton & Masciadrelli, 2013; Pfeiffer, 2007).

"Violence is an integral part of prison life. It is primarily a by-product of confining a large number of people with antisocial tendencies or behavior in close and frequently overcrowded quarters characterized by material and social deprivation" (Blitz, Wolff, & Shi, 2008, p. 385). In addition to the general nature of prison violence, Pare and Logan (2011) offer perspectives on why individuals with MHDs are likely to be victimized in prison. Regardless of if it is because of their mental illness, the stigma associated with that mental illness, or the physical display of symptoms, the results are inconclusive when it comes to determining if individuals with MHDs are more likely to be victimized in a correctional setting (Pare & Logan, 2011). Competing studies suggest that individuals with MHDs are more likely to be victimized (Blitz, Wolff, & Shi, 2008), *some but not all* MHDs are subjected to increased rates of victimization (Jachimowski, 2018b), and there is no increased likelihood of victimization for PwMI (Pare & Logan, 2011). However, there is a general consensus that individuals who have, or display symptoms of, significant psychological disorders (such as schizophrenia) are more likely to be victimized during their incarceration (Blitz, Wolff, & Shi, 2008; Jachimowski, 2018b; Pare & Logan, 2011). Victimization in prison can come at the hands of other inmates who react violently to the PwMI's atypical behavior. For example, Jachimowski (2018b) found that when an individual had *any* MHD, they were more likely to be intentionally injured or victimized since admission to the facility. And the same is as true for CO reactions: as Blitz, Wolff, and Shi (2008) reported, when an inmate exhibits a mental illness, the rate of staff-on-inmate physical victimization is 28.3 per capita, compared to 23.5 per capita when an inmate lacks a mental health diagnosis. This lack of training serves only to aggravate the PwMI's conditions, and ultimately leads to an increase in their risk of victimization.

COs are undoubtedly indispensable when it comes to the security and safety of prisons and jails (Kois, Hill, Gonzales, Hunter, & Chauhan, 2020). Antonio, Young, and Wingeard (2009) report that COs feel they have more responsibility when it comes to monitoring, correcting, and responding to inmates with MHDs compared to the mental health staff. Additionally, inmates with MHDs required more attention, different approaches/strategies for behavioral management, and more discretion than those without a MHD (Koi et al., 2020). If this is true, it stands to reason that COs *should* have significant training to engage and interact with these inmates. Unfortunately, the training that COs receive is exceedingly limited when it comes to working with inmates who have MHDs.

Of course, there are some strategies which serve as an alternative to traditional responses to inmates who have MHDs. One approach which uses both informal and formal intervention strategies (Dvoskin & Spiers, 2004), including formalized appointments with clinical personnel or specific, policy-based interventions from COs. Parker (2009) suggests a general mental health training which lasts two hours and covers symptoms, diagnoses, and how to respond to inmates with MHD. Beyond just mental health training, some researchers have suggested even using crisis intervention teams (CIT) training for COs (Davidson, 2016; Jachimowski & Smathers, 2019; Kerle, 2016; Kois et al., 2020). Unfortunately, as with most of the findings regarding the appropriate responses to mental health in the criminal justice system, the effectiveness of CIT in a prison setting is inconclusive. In theory, it appears a promising solution to successfully respond to individuals with MHDs and decrease violence interactions (Kerle, 2016; Kois et al., 2020) but in practice, it falls short (Jachimowski & Smathers, 2019). Unfortunately, there is a lack of rigorous research in this area of effective strategies for COs to respond to individuals with MHDs. One thing is certain, though, "'treatment' in corrections take many forms, perhaps the most important of which is basic human respect and concern" (Dvoskin & Spiers, 2004, p. 47).

Chapter 3

Mental Health's Implications for Policing

As deinstitutionalization and the criminalization of mental illness gave rise to an influx of individuals with MHDs entering the criminal justice system, police officers felt "that [they were] inheriting the problems of psychological services" (McLean & Marshall, 2010). By the 1980s, the U.S. government doubled down on these philosophies by decreasing funding to community-based mental health centers and closing state-run mental health institutions at a more rapid pace. In the end, this served to only exacerbate the problems that stemmed from the initial deinstitutionalization efforts, including homelessness, substance abuse, and being policed for minor criminal infractions. This was partially due to how the monies were being used; rather than being funneled toward mental health facilities (state-run or community-based), they were allocated to the newly declared "war on drugs" (Humphreys & Rappaport, 1993). This resulted in considerable political fear mongering and newly passed tough-on-drugs legislation (Moore & Elkavich, 2008). Subsequently, laws concerning homelessness, substance abuse, and drug enforcement contributed to an increase in the number of arrests of individuals with mental illness, furthering the disproportionality that such individuals entered into the justice system (Lurigio, 2013).

Research has consistently shown that PwMIs are arrested (and convicted) more frequently, net of controls, than the general public (Skeem et al., 2011; Vinkers, de Beurs, Barendregt, Rinne, & Hoek, 2011). In this chapter, we extend the conversation from the preceding chapter explicitly into the realm of policing. Therefore, it considers the criminalization of mental illness and its consequences for police officers and police agencies. It concludes a theoretical framework to understand these relationships, preparatory for the second half of the book.

POLICE AND INDIVIDUALS WITH MENTAL ILLNESS

Given the criminalization of mental illness, it is no surprise that police officers act not only as gatekeepers for the criminal justice system but can also be
understood to be in the same role for the mental health system (cf. Jennings
& Hudak, 2005). The difficulty with this setup, however, is that police simply
do not possess the training, nor are there informed policies or appropriate
procedures for officers to adequately engage in such a role (cf. Ruiz & Miller,
2004). This has resulted, among other things, in a rise in the disproportionate
number of arrests (and subsequent incarceration) of individuals with mental
illness. Policy makers, researchers, and police administrators have taken note
of this increasing trend.

Indeed, as Akins and colleagues noted in a 2014 study, although PwMI
make up roughly 5 percent of the general population, they constitute between
7 and 10 percent of all police–civilian contacts (Akins, Burkhardt, & Lanfear,
2014). Although some researchers may disagree with these numbers (as noted
by Akins and colleagues), none disagree that such disparity exists. And a
related concern is the disproportionate number of PwMI who have *repeated*
contacts with the police. As Akins and colleagues point out, nearly half of
all individuals with repeated police contact in a two-month time period were
PwMI. We consider two specific concerns regarding police-PwMI interactions before turning to divisionary strategies: police perceptions and interactions when responding to what we are calling *mental* health calls for service
(MHCFS); and police use of force against PwMI.

Police Perceptions and Interactions
When Responding to MHCFS

Police response to civilian behavior is in large part determined by policy and
precinct norms (Klinger, 1997). Police behavior can also be influenced by
their degree of confidence in such policies and norms. That is, a police officer's behavior in any given situation is in part informed by how comfortable
or confident they are in the administrative policies that guide their discretion.
An officer who is more confident in what the policies demand of them are
likely to make decisions more appropriate to the situation than an officer who
lacks such confidence (Ruiz & Miller, 2004). To that point, Bittner (1967)
observed over fifty years ago and Engel and Silver (2011) more recently,
police have little to no confidence in the policies that guide their discretion
when it comes to an individual with a MHD, even as they accept working
with individuals who have a MHD as part of their professional expectations.
This lack of confidence is further exacerbated by feelings among the police
that any ultimate decisions about where individuals with MHDs should

go—the criminal justice or the mental health systems—should *not* lie with them (McLean & Marshall, 2010).

McLean and Marshall (2010) approach officer response to MHCFS using qualitative methods to extract key phrase and frustrations presented by the officers. One of the biggest frustrations faced by police officers in their study was feeling as though their role was being misused *or* that there were no successful outcome options. Though officers overall responded with compassion and the "want to be able to help more" perspective, they reported that at times they received criticisms or minimal support from mental health care workers when presenting an individual in crisis (Jennings & Hudak, 2005).

As Sellers and colleagues (2005), among others, have pointed out, the exact role of police vis-à-vis PwMI is rather unclear. Although a role that interacts with PwMI regularly may cohere with the concept of community problem-solving (although there is even a reasonable argument against this coherence), it chafes against the traditional role of the police as peacekeepers and enforcers of law. Consider the two solutions officers have when responding to a MHCFS: a legalistic approach or response increases the likelihood that an officer will arrest or involuntarily commit an individual, whereas a problem-solving strategy would be used to find a long-term solution, even if the outcome is informal (Jennings & Hudak, 2005).

Thus, under a community problem-solving context, the role of the police would be assisting PwMI to find and utilize mental health care facilities, effectively making them gatekeepers to the mental health care system. Despite this framework, however, police generally have no real guidelines (be it training or policies to recommend individuals to mental health facilities) on how to work with PwMI and get them to the mental health system. This conundrum is driven by the fact that police, by policy and disposition, will default to immediate public safety, which typically means arrest (Ruiz & Miller, 2004). Once this occurs, the criminal justice system—as far as the police are concerned—has taken over. Simply, officers who approach MHCFS from a "law enforcer" position tend to be more motivated to maintain their authority via arrest (Markowitz & Watson, 2015).

This is most common whenever the PwMI presents aggressive behavior toward the police (or other civilians). Ruiz and Miller (2004) outline five such possible scenarios to which escalation might occur: the PwMI's fear of being in an unfamiliar situation with unknown individuals; lack of cooperation from the PwMI upon police commands because of the PwMI's diagnosis; the police officer's lack of training or even compassion; the PwMI's fearful reaction to a police officer's commanding demeanor; and the officer's fear for their personal safety. These triggers can result not only in arrest or, at the least, custody, but also in the police employing force against the PwMI.

With regard to individuals with MHDs being fearful of the police, Mclean and Marshall (2010) reported the officers interviewed recognized the potential impact their (the officer's) presence would have on the individual. In one case the officer is quoted as saying, "[p]art of the problem we get with mental health issues, people can react badly to seeing a police officer in uniform . . . they don't like it and they get frightened . . . is it fair to them; probably not" (McLean & Marshall, 2010, p. 66). Similarly, Livingston and colleagues (2014a) reported an individual who had a MHD suggested firing police officers who were refusing to educate themselves on mental illness because "[y]ou can't keep on people who are going to abuse people with mental illnesses" (p. 338). Finally, we would be remised if we did not take a moment to recognize the importance and role of procedural justice when officers make decisions regarding MHCFS. Similar to the general population, when individuals with MHDs felt they were approached and processed in a just manner they were less likely to have negative feelings and escalated behaviors, whereas coercive or threatening officer actions reduced the feelings of perceived procedural justice (Livingston et al., 2014b). More to that point, Watson, Angell, Vidalon, and Davis (2010) report officers who attempt to use threats or coercion to gain control of the situation can lead to an increased likelihood of violence.

In addition to the compliance of PwMI, officer's perceptions play a vital role in how a situation evolves or devolves once the officer arrives on the scene. Through misinformation via the media, the stigma surrounding mental illness, and a lack of training, officers may be more likely to perceive danger in an environment in which a PwMI is showing symptoms of their MHD and/or being none compliant to commands (Cappellazzo, 2016). Again, it is important to note that training can help an officer by providing them with skills to approach situations using nonviolent responses. Officers can arrive on the scene without the ability to identify mental health symptoms, respond effectively, or de-escalate the situation which leads to an increased level of force (Cappellazzo, 2016); and an increased level of violence and aggression (Livingston et al., 2014a).

Police Use of Force against Individuals with Mental Illness

Even though police rarely employ physical force during encounters with civilians (less than 1 percent of all interactions involve such force, cf. Morabito et al., 2010), the fact that police must invoke physical force at all in a democratic society is at the heart of the paradox of policing in the United States. And even leaving that philosophical—but no less pertinent—discussion aside, police use of force warrants discussion, generally, and specifically when it comes to PwMI. As discussed above, PwMI are often more prone to be recipients of police officer use of force because the individuals with MHDs often display behavior that can reasonably be construed as uncooperative at best and confrontational—even deadly—at worst. Civilian demeanor in tandem with behavior are the primary predictors of police use of force (Morabito et al., 2010; Taheri, 2014), both of which can be exacerbated by suspect/ civilian mental impairment.

Because the number one etiological covariate for police use of force has to do with the dangerous, or perceived dangerous, behavior of the civilian, it is perhaps not surprising that PwMI—whose behavior can at times be reasonably construed as dangerous, to themselves, the officer, and the public— would regularly be the target of police use of force (Morabito & Socia, 2015). The literature is not, however, unambiguous on the actual (or even perceived) danger of PwMI. For example: while Johnson (2011) found that an individual diagnosed with psychotic or personality disorders, were more likely (than non-PwMI counterparts) to exhibit behavior perceived as threatening toward police officers; whereas Kesic, Thomas, and Ogloff (2010) found the exact opposite. Namely, it was those without a mental illness who were more likely to exhibit violent behavior toward police officers. Such contradictory research reflects the very real contradictory lived experience of police officers, which further clouds their trust in departmental policies on how to interact with an individual who has a MHD. With a lack of support, understanding, and training, officers find themselves in positions where they are functioning as a reaction to the environment, leading to improper decisions, including reacting violently or processing individuals through the criminal justice system instead of the mental health system (Sellers et al., 2005).

DIVERSION STRATEGIES AND THE RISE OF CIT

Although police departments (and certainly police officers) were essaying to adjust their policies and behavior vis-à-vis PwMI since deinstitutionalization, it was not until the 1990s that they began to truly reevaluate, in any systemic sense, their role in the community in this specific domain. As discussed by Borum and colleagues (1998), three types of responses were developed at this time, which they categorized in the following ways: police-based specialized police response, police-based specialized mental health response, and mental health-based specialized mental health response. For each of these approaches, the emphasis changed in terms of who took the lead in encounters with PwMI as well as the direction in which the encounter was driven.

First, in some localities, police are given authority to lead the decision-making process. Under such *police-based specialized police responses*, the police receive mental health training in order to adequately assume this role. It is under this category that we find crisis intervention teams (CIT), which will be discussed in more detail, presently. We would like to note that mental health training and CIT training are not the same. Under *police-based specialized mental health responses*, mental health officials, one employed by the police agency but who, themselves, are not sworn police officers, typically take the lead in interactions with PwMIs. Most notably, under *mental health-based specialized mental health response*, a team of mental health providers and police officers collaborate during any MHCFS. A typical example of such a framework includes what have become known as *mobile crisis teams* (Borum, Deane, Steadman, & Morrissey, 1998). Most notably, the "Crisis Outreach and Support Team (COAST)" based out of Albuquerque is a great example of a *police-based specialized mental health response*, which we discuss each of these in more depth below.

Crisis Intervention Teams

The ultimate goal of CITs since their inception has been to decrease the level of violence inherent in encounters involving police and PwMI (Compton, Broussard, Reed, Crisafio, & Watson, 2015). At the heart of CIT is training for officers to serve as a liaison between the initial responder to MHCFS and the mental health system. Such training includes a multitude of topics, including the nature of mental health disorders; availability of local resources for the mentally ill; laws pertaining to PwMI and crime, *inter alia* (Taheri, 2014). While the concept of *crisis intervention* began just after the Revolutionary War ended during the Whiskey Rebellion of 1794, the implementation, strategy, and application have continued to evolve to suit societal issues in the United States (Harmening, 2014).

The Albuquerque Police Department (APD) modeled their CIT after the creation of the Memphis CIT. In 1999, more than five out-of-state police departments graduated from the Albuquerque program, and at the time the CIT made up one-fourth of the field patrol (Bowers & Pettit, 2001). Despite the age of the evaluation and the increased use of CIT in the modern police department, it is important to review one of the first CIT evaluations. Overall Bower and Pettit (2001) report that there were impressive results after gathering three years' worth of data regarding the effectiveness of the Albuquerque program. At that time, the CIT responded to more than 3,200 calls and transported individuals with a MHD to a mental health facility in just under half of those calls. Additionally, just over 1 percent of the calls resulted in an injury to the civilian (Bower & Pettit, 2001). Officers were specifically selected to be a part of the APD CIT after showing that they possessed superior communication, problem-solving, and tactical skills. More so, after being selected, these officers underwent intensive screening and evaluations to determine eligibility to the next phase of enrollment (Bower & Pettit, 2011): the forty-hour curriculum. Such training consisted of instructions on handling special populations, substance abuse, and case management while in the field. To decrease the turnover rate, CIT officers received an additional $50 incentive pay with their weekly salary. The researchers and department suggest that the success of the program stems from the dedication and the replication of other successful models and not to mention selection bias (Bower & Pettit, 2001).

A six-year longitudinal study was conducted between 1998 and 2004 in the Akron Police Department. During this time, there were more than 1.5 million calls for service, 10,000 of which were calls for service reported as "related to mental disturbances" (Teller, Munetz, Gil, & Ritter, 2006). There were seven actions which an officer was likely to respond: transport to psychiatric services; transports to other treatment facilities; arrest and transport to jail; formal interaction where transport to jail was unnecessary; transportation to another location; no police interaction and actions which were taken but are unknown (Teller et al., 2006). Ritter, Teller, Marcussen, Munetz, and Teasdale (2011) conducted a study based on the characteristics of the officer dispatch team in Seattle, Washington (the Seattle Police Department) to determine if there was a relationship between the dispatchers and the action officers would take once they arrived on scene. To this end, researchers gathered official records on the interactions between police officers once arriving on the scene, the coding process of the call, and the interaction between dispatch and the officers (Ritter et al., 2011). Ritter et al. (2011) analyzed 2,174 officer reports when the officer described responding to a call for service and interacted with a person perceived to have a mental illness. Foregoing the level of training the responding officer possessed, the models' (likelihood of transportation) were different depending on whether the call was specific about a mental illness (more likely to be transported to a treatment facility) or the way in which the call was dispatched (Ritter et al., 2011). Their results indicate that there are unknown variables regarding officer response when examining whether an individual assessment from a CIT (on-scene) is related to the dispatch code; and, consequently, whether the person was transported to jail or a treatment facility.

Modern-day CIT has three important goals: to return individuals in crisis back to a state of equilibrium; to remediate any damage experienced during the crisis; and to use resources efficiently to reduce the likelihood of another crisis (Harmening, 2014). The training and subsequent field skills rely on officers and cadets self-selecting themselves into CIT to focus on de-escalation of the situation and outsourcing those individuals to the appropriate resource (Reuland, Draper, & Norton, 2013). In more technical terms, officers should respond using the same five steps to intervening during a crisis: response, containment, de-escalation, remediation, and prevention.

Generally, research evaluating the effectiveness of CIT is very positive. This has been found across time and place, for example, during the late 1990s in Albuquerque (Bower & Pettit, 2001); between 1998 and 2004 in Akron (Teller et al., 2006); and Seattle in the first decade of the twentieth century (Ritter et al., 2011). Watson and colleagues' 2010 study is illustrative: departments with CIT, or officers with CIT training, were more likely to divert PwMIs from the justice system to the mental health system. The important caveat in Watson and colleagues' study—and most of the research on CIT—is that the impact of CIT on the use of force is somewhat inconclusive. Specifically, demeanor and behavior are still more likely to influence an officer's use of force after controlling for mental illness. It is therefore somewhat difficult to discern whether CIT actually "works" in any definitive manner. This conclusion must also be tempered due to methodological challenges (which are hardly unique to CIT research), such as the inability to isolate comparison groups, to simulate experimental settings, or the inability to tease out spuriousness in understanding police officer behavior (cf. Bower & Pettit, 2001; Helfgott, Hickman, & Labossiere, 2016; Ritter et al., 2011; Teller et al., 2006; Watson et al., 2008).

Mobile Crisis Team Approach

Mobile Crisis Teams (MCTs) were created in part as a response to the equivocal research surrounding CIT (Rosenbaum, 2010; Watson et al., 2008). MCTs, variously known as *mobile crisis units* (cf. Lord & Bjerregaard, 2014), *mobile crisis partnerships* (cf. Kisely et al., 2010), *crisis outreach* (cf. Cornelius et al., 2003), and *mobile response units* (Lee et al., 2015), are typically composed of law enforcement officers and clinicians. A MCT framework provides responding officers access to clinicians upon receiving a MHCFS. The clinician arrives as soon as possible to assess the PwMI during the initial police encounter (see Murphy [2012] for a more complete description of how MCTs are organized and function). It is often the case that MCTs and CIT-based responses are blurred, insofar as CIT officers are often trained to involve clinicians during a MHCFS (cf. Murphy, 2012). In any case, the MCT approach has generally made positive impressions on officers and PwMI alike (Kisely et al., 2010).

Most MCT consisted of police officers and clinicians, although the makeup of personnel was contingent on whether the program design allowed the clinician to respond with the officer (Lee et al., 2015), or if the clinician arrived after the officer requested an assessment (Murphy, 2012). In an Australian study of MCT, police officers reported being largely in favor of approaching the MHCFS with a clinician (Lee et al., 2015). Over the six-month pilot study of the MCT integration, MCT reported 296 contacts through the A-PACER (a variation of the original Police and Clinical Early Response). Out of those 296 contacts, 33 percent of individuals threatened suicide, 22 percent had welfare concerns (MCT needed to respond to issues with housing, welfare, substance treatment, or primary care services), and 18 percent were due to psychotic episodes. After the initial contact, 49 percent of individuals needed transportation from the original site, of which police officers were the most likely to transport the individual (58 percent) (Lee et al., 2015).

Kisely et al. (2010) focused their study on a pre- and post-evaluation of a MCT between policing services and a mental health team in Nova Scotia, Canada. The argument was, at the time of publication, that limited formal evaluations had been completed, and there was a need for a control group in a comparable area which did not have a MCT. Overall, during the three-year period of time during the study, the MCT saw an increase of approximately four times the number of calls for service in which the MCT responded between year 1 and year 3 (464 responses in year 1 and 1,666 responses in year 3). During this time, officers and clinicians were able to respond more quickly to calls for service, and the amount of time needed on the scene (Kisely et al., 2010).

Finally, specific to the United States, Lord and Bjerregaard (2014) found that officers who participated in a MCT were more likely to divert individuals from their original location to another location if they were male, intoxicated, and more likely to draw the attention of officers. Additionally, Lord and Bjerregaard (2014) report that without immediate intervention from mental health resources, officers may resort to physical restraint and arrest. Although the studies that have been done evaluating the effectiveness of MCT seem to be positive, it is difficult to discern the level of effectiveness. This is because the current studies vary on the aspects being evaluated and the limited number of studies (Lord & Bjerregaard, 2014). Lee and colleagues (2015) report at the time of their publication, only six studies had been completed across multiple countries since 1992; of those evaluations, only three had been completed more recently in 2010 or sooner.

As with CIT, so too with the overall research on the impact/effectiveness of MCT: while research exists that supports a decrease in arrest and violence during MHCFS under a MCT framework when compared to non-MCT MHCFS (e.g., Steadman, Deane, Borum, & Morrissey, 2000; Lord & Bjerregaard, 2014), other studies failed to find any differences of substance (e.g., Steadman, Cocozza, & Veysey, 1999; Scott, 2000). Again, as with CIT, there are salient methodological challenges to all of these MCT studies, which limit our ability to make conclusive statements as to their effectiveness (Lord & Bjerregaard, 2014; Lee et al., 2015; Kisely et al., 2010). For both

CIT and MCT, therefore, we would argue that the research is limited, yet promising, and that both CIT and MCT are a step in a better direction than traditional law enforcement responses to PwMI (read: simple arrest).

Community Crisis Specialists

"Community crisis specialists" and "street-psychologists" are coined phrases from the 1990s to describe individuals who are hired by police departments to respond to MHCFS; thus, allowing officers to reconsider their role in the community (Borum et al., 1998; Rosenbaum, 2010). The focus on shifting total responsibility from police officers to sharing responsibility mental health care providers stems from the "quiet revolution" that was community-based and problem-solving policing models (Borum et al., 1998, p. 394). Though there are many programs which employee mental health care staff in some capacity, it is most likely to function as a MCT, liaison for resources, or to provide mental health training to officers. It is far less likely that an agency has a program designed for responders who are not sworn officers.

The Birmingham Police Department created a *Community Service Officer* (CSO) program more than forty years ago which were civilian police tasked to respond to crisis calls and, in some cases, follow-up assistance (Borum et al., 1998; Steadman, Deane, Borum, & Morrissey, 2000). More than 50 percent of the CSOs surveyed reported feeling prepared to respond to MHCFS but, on average, paled in comparison to feelings of officer preparedness who were a part of a CIT or MCT program (100 percent and 78.1 percent, respectively). The Albuquerque *Crisis Outreach and Support Team* (COAST) differs from the Birmingham CSOs in structure but not concept. COAST employs civilians with a background in social work and case management to be available if, and when, officers request them at the scene (Rosenbaum, 2010). Similar to the Birmingham CSOs, COAST workers are responsible for follow-up interactions and proactive visits to homeless individuals to encourage them to use the resources available to them (Rosenbaum, 2010).

Unfortunately, given the ever-increasing robust literature surrounding CIT, MCT, and the potential danger associated with non-sworn officers responding to a call for service, most evaluations of police-based specialized mental health responses lack in rigor and conclusiveness. Following the same pattern as the two aforementioned programs, the studies which have been published appear to suggest that this could be a promising approach (Keown, Tacchi, Miemiec, & Hughes, 2007; Richman, Wilson, Scally, Edwards, & Wood, 2003; Rosenbaum, 2010; Steadman et al., 2000). One point, which is beyond the scope of this book would be the consideration of perceived effectiveness of these programs from the general population and the officers, despite a lack of empirical support.

THEORETICAL THOUGHTS

Having laid out the history of PwMI and the American justice system, in addition to its application specifically to the police, we now consider explanations underlying both CIT and MCT, with specific focus on CIT. Our book is not concerned *per se* with theory testing; but our thoughts and narrative in the forthcoming chapters are appropriately guided by three distinct theoretical frameworks: *Peplau's Theory of Interpersonal Relations*, *Structural Holes* and *Weak Ties*, and *Systems Theory*. We believe that these three theories, taken together, create a compelling guide for how police should approach MHCFS and other interactions with MHD, given the current criminalization of mental illness and the continual efforts at deinstitutionalization, in light of the current organizational paradigms of CIT/MCT. We discuss these theories' tenants and empirical support below, and then consider them again more fully in the final chapter with respect to our exploration of police officer training and in-service vis-à-vis individuals with MHDs/MHCFS.

Peplau's Theory of Interpersonal Relations

Peplau's Theory of Interpersonal Relations (TIR) was initially designed to explain and guide relationships between nurses and clients (cf. Peplau, 1997). More specifically, and as Peplau (1992) herself has indicated, it is particularly useful in directing the behavior of nurses vis-à-vis individuals with MHDs with SMI and most specifically for psychiatric nurses. Again, as we have noted elsewhere, while those with SMIs make up a relatively small portion of the general population, they are overrepresented among both homeless populations (25 to 33 percent, Davis et al., 2012) and among the incarcerated population (16 percent, Torrey et al., 2010). In other words, the very PwMI with whom police are most likely to work with. Indeed, TIR is especially suited to the police for at least one other reason: as Peplau (1997) has outlined it, nurse–client relationships are almost always quite short. In addition, it is the initial phase of the relationship—the so-called Orientation phase, which we describe presently—and is arguably the most important for the relationship, as it lays a considerable amount of groundwork in an abbreviated period of time. All of this describes the hallmarks of a police–civilian encounter. We expand on the applicability of TIR to the police in a moment; first, though, it remains to outline what TIR actually says.

As Peplau developed it, TIR suggests that nurse–client relationships revolve around the former's efforts to reduce the exogenous needs of the latter. Key to understanding this theory is the *interpersonal* nature of the relationship: the nurse and the client are thrust into a relationship that transcends the professional because of the very nature of needs required by the client. This is to say there is a difference in the level of intimacy between the nurse–client relationship and the car dealer–client relationship. While the latter involves a monetary transaction, the former involves not only fiduciary considerations but also deeply emotional elements tied to health and well-being. The intimacy inherent in the nurse–client relationship undergirds what Peplau describes as four sequential phases, namely: orientation, identification, exploitation, and resolution. As we've indicated, Peplau argues (and we agree) that the orientation phase is the most important in the sense that it is here that the relationship originates: the client makes his/her problem known to the nurse, and then the interlocution shifts to the nurse themselves, who identifies the most appropriate service. This takes place in a nebulous give-and-take, as more information is revealed, and a potential resolution is collaboratively developed. It is at this phase that the traditional approach to MHCFS stop for the police: following their training, they assess the severity of the threat, and respond with either detention or diversion. CIT offers more than this, however, as we shall explain.

The second phase, identification, involves seeking out professional assistance most appropriate to the clients' needs. This phase has the potential to empower the client, reducing feelings of confusion, anxiety, and helplessness. This is followed by the exploitation phase, where the client, nurse, and professional all work toward a solution collaboratively. This process might be described as "trial-and-error," but only in the sense that the three entities (client, nurse, and professional) work together to tease out the best possible way to meet the client's needs and to implement it wholly. It is appropriate to describe the exploitation phase as "problem-solving" in the same sense police departments employ the term, a la Goldstein (1990). Finally, Peplau describes the resolution phase as the end of the nurse–client relationship. This termination is the result of the patient's needs having been collaboratively met. There is an evaluative substratum to this phase for both the client and the nurse in terms of both the success of the process and of the outcome.

What does TIR mean for the police? We have already touched lightly on its application for guiding police during MHCFS. We believe, however, that TIR has the potential to offer even more for law enforcement officers within the context of CIT. At a simplistic, albeit important level, TIR emphasizes the importance of both verbal and nonverbal communication skills. CIT officers are typically chosen for their superior communication skills (Bower & Pettit, 2011). Thus, even at this seemingly obvious level, TIR becomes a potentially important tool for the police to use during MHCFS. Less obvious but perhaps more important is that TIR focuses the nurse on explicitly "[taking] an investigative approach that does not avoid exploring stressful situations but rather focuses upon the problems the person is experiencing" (Thelander, 1997, p. 26). This is key to improving officer-PwMI encounters insofar as the focus shifts from the traditional just desserts/deterrence model of criminal justice to one that is focused on problem-solving—something that police are already prepared to engage in. We believe, then, that TIR can be fruitfully employed by the police to guide their interactions with individuals with MHDs from one that is best described as order maintenance to one that is understood to be problem-solving, but doing so within the context of mental health needs and services.

Structural Holes and Weak Ties

Given that the strength of CIT lays not with officers "knowing it all," but ultimately with officers' awareness of a network composed of salient persons, we believe that social networking theories also hold great promise for MHCFS. We focus particularly on Burt's (1992) theory of structural holes and Granovetter's (1973) theory of weak ties as applied by Scott and Carrington's (2011) social networking framework. To start, Burt suggested in any given institutional environment, success is more likely predicated on *who* one knows rather than *what* one knows. Rather than describing despotism or a Carnegian approach to relationships, Burt is saying that for any given person to know *everything* is ultimately an inefficient waste of resources. Rather, institutions should invest in what he calls "players" with diverse capital: financial capital, human capital, and social capital. Financial capital is the amount of money, lines of credit, and monetary reserve that an individual possesses whereas human capital is attributional characteristics such as intelligence, charisma, and health, and social capital is comprised of the relationships a player creates and from which she can draw financial and human capital (Burt, 1992).

It is this latter capital that is most closely related to Granovetter's theory of weak ties, which postulates that an institution's strength is determined not by how strong its ties to other institutions is (or, as Burt would call them, players) but with how many times they possess that lack redundancy. This is because ties that are strong are typically between homogenous players; therefore, what each player brings to the table will ultimately mirror one another. For example a police department with line officers who patrol in Ford Crown Victorias will have little to gain in its relationship with another police department with line officers who patrol in Dodge Chargers: there is a redundancy of resources and institutional knowledge. But a police department with line officers who patrol in Ford Rangers has much to gain in developing a relationship—however nominal—with a hospital or a school. Although Burt (1992) has argued that there is a difference between structural holes and weak ties theories (based on the empirical potential, or lack thereof, of each theory), Scott and Carrington (2011) compellingly argue the difference is ultimately one of semantics: both theories argue that connecting to multiple—and seemingly disparate—institutions best positions an organization to more effectively and efficiently make decisions, because they are exposed to more information with less redundancy, and because they are exposed to more "tools" than they themselves may possess.

In the context of our book, these social networking approaches underlie why police should not be burdened alone with the care of an individual with a MHD, but should instead invest in creating networks from the mental health service community. This will ease the burden of responsibility on the shoulders of all parties, while providing a meaningful and collaborative relationship that, as TIR would predict, would be better able to meet the needs of all those involved: the public, the police, the PwMI, and any other actors involved in the MHCFS.

Systems Theory

Perhaps no other model of criminal justice has had more of an impact on how we understand the justice system than the systems model (Klofas, Hipple, & McGarrell, 2010). First applied to the criminal justice "system" in the 1960s, in response to the five hot long summers of race riots and composing a major part of the report *The Challenge of Crime in a Free Society*, it has remained with criminal justice students ever since. It's immortalized in the "fishbone" diagram so regularly printed in the frontispiece of introductory textbooks as to be benign. While the systems model is not without its critics (e.g., Packer's [1964] dual taxonomy model and Walker's [1994] wedding-cake and administrative models of criminal justice, as described in each edition of his invaluable *Sense and Nonsense about Crime and Drugs* volume), it remains at the back of the mind of every student and practitioner of the justice system. Importantly, it demonstrates just how each part of the criminal justice system (police, courts, corrections) is related to one another, as well as provides opportunities for diversion away from the justice system. Where we believe that the systems model is most applicable is in expanding the definition of system from the closed environment employed by the 1960s version to a more open model, where the justice system is merely part of a larger sociopolitical ecology.

This notion has been discussed since at least the 1990s. For example, Morgan in 1998 argued that any organizational environment must work with other organizational environments, and that this inevitably creates a system that, in turn, renders the shared environment more manageable. Similarly, Coleman and Cotton (2010) noted that in any shared environment, if one system changes, other systems will also be affected, no matter the size of the change. And as Amagoh (2008) has suggested, no institution is truly independent. Trite, but true: society is as ecological as a wetland.

So, what does this mean for the police? Quite a bit, as our discussion of deinstitutionalization and criminalization of mental illness has demonstrated (cf. Vaughan [2011], for a more complete discussion on this matter). But moving forward, the open systems approach, we believe, also offers something to guide police behavior vis-à-vis PwMI. The question is not *should* or *do* the criminal justice and mental health systems collaborate, but in *what manner*. Systems theory provides a framework for making decisions that involve interdependent systems, something that describes the current CIT paradigm that we consider in our volume. As Steward and Ayres (2010) have noted, interdependent systems can only move toward shared goals if they actually work in tandem, rather than independently of each other.

CONCLUSIONS

We have endeavored in this chapter to outline the implications of deinstitutionalization as it applied to the police. The corpus of research on this topic is consonant: deinstitutionalization leads irresistibly to the criminalization of mental illness, with the ultimate result of the police interacting more frequently with PwMI. Such interactions have often been, at best, unnecessary, or, at worst, fatal (for either party, or third parties). Unlike *the Challenge of Crime in a Free Society*, we do not lay the blame at the feet of the police in any general sense. Police are limited by the tools available to them: search, seize, disperse, divert. Given the nature of police officer encounters with an individual with a MHD described above, it is often the case that the police reasonably only have recourse to *seize* when responding to MHCFS. As police themselves will readily admit, this approach is ineffective. Something new is required.

The approaches of CIT and MCT are two such potential "something news": each rightly involves the police in responding to MHCFS but does so with specific training and with collaborative relationships with other service providers. The nature of both this training and collaborations is one of the same immediacy inherent in any police officer response to a call for service. We suggest the strength of these two approaches is that they are not haphazard, knee-jerk reactions to a politically perceived social problem, but are instead substantiated by at least three empirically supported theories: TIR, social networks, and systems. Each theory complements or fills out the bones of the other theories, meaning that, together, they present a picture that is not too broad yet remains comprehensive; do not suggest one-size-fits-all solutions, but rather embrace the problem-oriented/intelligence-led policing models popular today among departments; and draw on the strengths of each party involved in the collaborative relationship rather than requiring a single party to "know it all."

We will have much more to say about what these theories actually mean for police response to MHCFS in chapter 6. But we wanted to lay the groundwork *here* to ensure that the conversation moves forward with these three theoretical guides in the background. At this point in our volume, we proceed with a consideration of how CIT training is employed/perceived among police officers across two specific points of tenure: the academy and the job itself.

Part II

STATE OF POLICING AND MENTAL HEALTH CALLS FOR SERVICE

Having discussed mental health, the police, and policing generally, we now turn to the current state of how police approach mental health calls for service. This section therefore considers two particular milieus of training familiar to all police: the academy and in-service. The focus is on training and how it affects the potential actions of police, both at the start of their careers and in the middle of them, vis-à-vis mental health calls for service. We conclude by reconsidering the theoretical frameworks we introduced in chapter 3 and flesh out their implications for the police and PwMI.

Chapter 4

Police Training

General Patterns Related to CIT

In this chapter, we consider general patterns of how police are trained relative to PwMI. (The next chapter reconsiders these patterns in light of more sophisticated statistical models.) To do so, we rely on our own observations among police academy cadets and police agencies across several states. (See appendices A, B, and C for details regarding our methodology, survey instrument, and vignette universe, respectively.) Importantly, we consider both academy training and in-service training, reflecting the training experiences of new and tenured officers.

WHOM ARE WE LOOKING AT?

In most respects, our participants reflect what might reasonably be considered an "average" American police officer, as illustrated in table 4.1. (This statement must, of course, be qualified that this national aggregation will mask the demographic make-up of specific American cities that defy this "norm.") For example, 91 percent of our respondents were male, and 92 percent were white/non-Latino (compared to 6 percent black, 1 percent Asian, 5 percent Latino, and 4 percent who indicated "Other"). Because of this racial/ethnic make-up, we opted to collapse our categories to reflect "white" and "non-white." We readily admit this is far from ideal, but those familiar with quantitative research methods will recognize its inherent analytical limitations. Finally, the age ranges of our sample were bimodally distributed, with 39 percent indicating that they were between the ages of 35 and 44 and another 39 percent indicating that they were between the ages of 45 and 54 (of the remaining categories, 13 percent were between 18 and 24; 32 percent

Table 4.1 Frequencies for Independent Variables

Variable	Valid n	Valid %	Variable	Valid n	Valid %
Sex			**CIT training**		
(0) = female	13	9.4	(0) = no	28	19.9
(1) = male	125	90.6	(1) = yes	112	80.1
Race			**Volunteered**		
(1) = African American	8	5.71	(0) = no	58	52.3
(2) = Asian	2	1.42	(1) = yes	53	47.4
(3) = Caucasian		92.14	**Professional**		
(4) = Latino	7	5	(0) = no	31	22.3
(5) = Other	6	4.29	(1) = yes	108	77.7
Race combined			**Family**		
(0) = White	124	88.57	(0) = no	65	46.6
(1) = Non-white	16	11.43	(1) = yes	75	53.4
Age			**Resource type**		
(1) = 18–24	13	9.3	type_CMHS	24	4.57
(2) = 25–34	32	23	type_MSNH	112	21.33
(3) = 35–44	39	27.7	type_OMH	74	14.10
(4) = 45–54	39	27.9	type_ORES	40	7.62
(5) = 55–64	16	11.4	type_PH	92	17.52
(6) = 65–74	1	0.7	type_PSY	112	21.33
Role			type_RTCA	71	13.53
(0) = cadet	27	19.1	**Vig_sex**		
(1) = police officer	114	80.9	(0) = female	353	50.1
Patrol area			(1) = male	352	49.9
(1) = urban	63	55.3	**Vig_diagnosis**		
(2) = suburban	36	31.6	(0) = intoxication	237	33.6
(3) = rural	15	13.1	(1) = mental health	468	66.4
Department size			**Vig_crime**		
(1) = small	26	23	(0) = ask for money	367	52.1
(2) = medium	53	46.9	(1) = act strangely	338	47.9
(3) = large	34	30.1	**Vig_compliance**		
Negative experience			(0) = responsive	361	51.2
(0) = No	28	25.2	(1) = unresponsive	344	48.8
(1) = Yes	83	74.8			

	$\bar{x}$	sd		$\bar{x}$	sd
Cadet weeks	8.72	2.91	**Resources**	12.52	15.55
Years officer	18.31	10.04			

between 25 and 34; 16 percent between 55 and 64; and a single respondent was between 65 and 74).

Of our 114 sworn law enforcement officers, the average number of years in service (*yearspolice*) was about 18 (*sd* ≈ 10), and a little over half were employed in what should be categorized as urban areas, compared to about one-third in suburban areas and 13 percent working in rural areas. These numbers are reasonably reflected in the respondent distribution of departmental sizes: about a quarter worked in "small" departments, a little under half worked in "medium" departments, and a little under a third worked in "large" departments. And of our twenty-seven police cadets, the average number of weeks in the academy was about 9 (*sd* $\approx$ 3). Across both the cadets and officers, the majority had received some form of CIT training (80 percent). For most, this was required—but it was a slim margin, with just under half volunteering for the training (48 percent).

In addition, because we are interested ultimately in what drives dispositional decisions during MHCFS, we also asked if the respondent knew a professional health care worker they could contact if they had questions, as well as if they had anyone in their family who suffered from a serious mental disorder. A full three-quarters did not have a professional they could call on during a call for service. A little over half had a family member who had been diagnosed with a serious mental illness (e.g., schizophrenia or severe depression).

Finally, we explored mental health resources that our respondents might have been aware were available for reference (see figure 4.1). To this end, we independently assessed which mental health resources existed within each police agency's jurisdiction. We included varying types of mental health facilities using the Substance Abuse and Mental Health Services Administration (SAMHSA) National Directory of Mental Health Treatment Facilities.

As table 4.1 demonstrates, some services were more available than others, specifically multi-setting mental health facilities and psychiatric hospitals/units. Hospitalization/day treatment centers were also common, and a little over half of the jurisdictions included either outpatient mental health facilities or residential treatment centers for adults. Only community mental health centers and other residential treatment facilities were limited (and the latter is more explainable in terms of being a "catch all" category).

Already, we can start to see the impact of deinstitutionalization for the police: there is no standard of care delivery across the board. Although we did not explore the quality of these services, we think it is fair to assume that just as there is no standard of delivery, there will also be variations in the quality of care. Certainly, such variation in quality would exist even if all such delivery methods were standardized. However, such variation would be due to say, personal perspectives, rather than issues in disparate funding, training, and benchmarks. For example, the officer's or cadet's personal opinion on mental health, the role of police, and close experience with individuals who have mental health disorders. We attempt to control for some of these personal

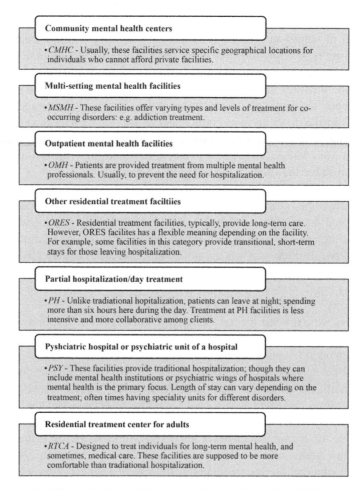

Community mental health centers

• *CMHC* - Usually, these facilities service specific geographical locations for individuals who cannot afford private facilities.

Multi-setting mental health facilities

• *MSMH* - These facilities offer varying types and levels of treatment for co-occurring disorders: e.g. addiction treatment.

Outpatient mental health facilities

• *OMH* - Patients are provided treatment from multiple mental health professionals. Usually, to prevent the need for hospitalization.

Other residential treatment faciltiies

• *ORES* - Residential treatment facilities, typically, provide long-term care. However, ORES facilites has a flexible meaning depending on the facility. For example, some facilities in this category provide transitional, short-term stays for those leaving hospitalization.

Partial hospitalization/day treatment

• *PH* - Unlike tradiational hopitalization, patients can leave at night; spending more than six hours here during the day. Treatment at PH facilities is less intensive and more collaborative among clients.

Pyshciatric hospital or psychiatric unit of a hospital

• *PSY* - These facilities provide traditional hospitalization; though they can include mental health institutions or psychiatric wings of hospitals where mental health is the primary focus. Length of stay can vary depending on the treatment; often times having speciality units for different disorders.

Residential treatment center for adults

• *RTCA* - Designed to treat individuals for long-term mental health, and sometimes, medical care. These facilities are supposed to be more comfortable than tradiational hospitalization.

Figure 4.1   Brief Descriptions and Acronyms of Mental Health Facilities.

perspectives with variables measuring interactions with family members who have a serious mental health disorder and respondents who have interacted with individuals with MHDs. While such standardized trainings and benchmarks do exist in terms of mental health care, not all of it is required beyond specific educational requirements and in-service trainings that are mostly geared toward safety and legal issues.

These potential negatives aside, there are also possible positives underlying the patterns concerning mental health services available in an officer's jurisdiction. For example, although it is not expressly indicated in table 4.1, *every* jurisdiction had *something* for mental health help. In fact, most had *multiple* options for police officers to harness. The real question, then, is if having these mental health facilities—and if having *more than one* such service provider—*matters* in terms of how the police approach MHCFS. This question is vitally important insofar as our observations bear out the frequency of contacts between the police and individuals with MHDs: of our 114 law enforcement officers, a full 101 have had to involuntarily commit someone (table 4.2). More concerning: of those 101 officers, a full four-fifths indicated the experience was negative.

TAKING A LOOK AT OUR OUTCOME OF INTEREST: POTENTIAL DISPOSITION

Vignette Responses

First, we felt it was important to provide examples of the vignettes used to evaluate whether officers would respond differently given certain character-istics of the scenario. The first vignette example was used as the template for all other vignettes (see figure 4.2). You can see that each vignette indicates a varying degree of mental health disorder symptoms and control variables. The second and third vignettes are scenarios (see figure 4.3) which were used during the survey period, after a pretest confirmed these were legitimate sce-narios which might occur.

Ultimately, we are interested in *how police are responding to mental health calls for service*. To this end, we asked our officers and cadets how they would reasonably respond to specific vignettes that featured a variety of variables associated with such calls. As explained in appendix A, we had a universe of twenty-four vignettes (see appendix C for full vignette universe). Our vignettes randomized a number of categories, such as the perceived diagnosis of the suspect, their gender, and the type of crime being commit-ted (see figure 4.2). Respondents could indicate one of four responses to each vignette: *arrest, involuntary commitment, informal resolution*, and *do nothing*.

The vignettes were randomly shown to participants at a rate of five vignettes per survey; these were very equally distributed and represented (see table 4.1 for frequency statistics). Across all twenty-four vignettes (for an

Table 4.2 Descriptive Statistics for Dependent Variables

Variable	Valid n	x̄	sd
% likely to arrest	705	20.39	23.40
% likely to involuntarily commit	705	51.67	31
% likely to informally resolve	705	27.48	28.35
% likely to do nothing	705	1.19	4.96

Base Vignette:

While you are on patrol you receive a call for service, the dispatcher relays that the caller indicated the individual has a mental illness. According to the caller, there is an individual who is (crime) and (diagnosis). When you arrive on the scene, you identify as a police officer and the (sex) is (compliance) to your commands. Using the following scale, how likely are you to do each of the following actions?

Vignette dimension and text:

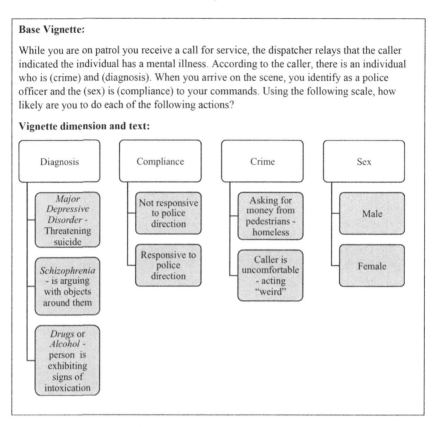

Figure 4.2   Creating the Vignettes.

example, see figure 4.3), arrest was chosen as the likely outcome on average 20 percent of the time; involuntary commitment was chosen 52 percent of the time; informal resolution 28 percent of the time; and do nothing was chosen 1 percent of the time (see table 4.2). In and of themselves, these first-order univariate statistics present a compelling picture of police officer behavior vis-à-vis individuals with MHDs. First, virtually *all of the time* police will do *something* when called to a MHCFS. This finding may seem trivial at first glance, but it is far from so. The hallmark of police discretion is not just *what* do police do but *if* they actually do anything. The fascinating finding of policing surveys throughout time, after all, is that police officers do not always make formal dispositions when they had every legal justification to do so. The question remains, of course, *what* are they doing?

From our survey, it appears that just over half of the time they are involuntarily committing someone who clearly displays some sort of serious mental

1. While you are on patrol you receive a call for service, the dispatcher relays that the caller indicated the individual has a mental illness. According to the caller, there is an individual who is acting strange and arguing with objects and appears to be hallucinating. When you arrive on the scene, you identify as a police officer and the male is unresponsive to your commands. Using the following scale, how likely are you to do each of the following actions?

0%	10%	20%	30%	40%	50%	60%	70%	80%	90%	100%
No Chance		Low Chance		Some Chance		Good Chance		High Chance		Completely Certain

Likelihood of arresting the person and transport them to your holding facility: _____

Likelihood of holding the person and seek to have them involuntarily committed: _____

Likelihood of an informal resolution at the scene (ie: conflict resolution, warning): _____

Likelihood of doing nothing and leaving the scene: _____

2. While you are on patrol you receive a call for service, the dispatcher relays that the caller indicated the individual has a mental illness. According to the caller, the individual is asking for money from pedestrians and is exhibiting signs of intoxication. When you arrive on the scene you identify as a police officer and the female is unresponsive to your commands. Using the following scale, how likely are you to do each of the following actions?

0%	10%	20%	30%	40%	50%	60%	70%	80%	90%	100%
No Chance		Low Chance		Some Chance		Good Chance		High Chance		Completely Certain

Likelihood of arresting the person and transport them to your holding facility: _____

Likelihood of holding the person and seek to have them involuntarily committed: _____

Likelihood of an informal resolution at the scene (ie: conflict resolution, warning): _____

Likelihood of doing nothing and leaving the scene: _____

Figure 4.3   Example Vignettes.

health diagnosis, compared to informal resolutions roughly a quarter of the time. These findings are somewhat promising, insofar as it means police are leaving the justice system itself as a sort of "last resort." (We did not actually tease out any ranking of choices, so we are using this turn of phrase rather loosely.) Rather, they are choosing to involve the mental health system at first explicitly—through involuntary commitment—and implicitly through "informal resolutions," which, of course, have a wide range, from involving counselors, to suggesting mental health assistance, to involving caretakers, *inter alia.* Either way, it is heartening to see that the justice system is not the first "go to" for the police in most situations involving MHCFS.

First-order correlations, presented in table 4.3, unveiled some fascinating relationships hidden in our univariate statistics, above. First, CIT training had a positive association with whether an officer/cadet would do nothing when called to a scene with an individual who potentially had a SMI MHD. Unfortunately, the coefficient's effect size was nominal ($r = 0.082$). More disheartening were the null results for the other categorical responses—arrest, involuntary commitment, or informal resolution. Similarly null results were discovered for the association between knowing someone professionally whom a police officer could call upon during a MHCFS, and having some-one in their family who has suffered from a SMI: in terms of the former, this did reduce the likelihood of arrest, but again at a rather nominal strength ($r = -0.095$); in terms of the latter, results were null across the board (see table 4.4).

Should these results cause us concern? Or, perhaps a more accurate ques-tion we can ask, do these results nullify our statements above regarding our zero-order findings? We think not. In explaining why, we feel this way, it is tempting to hide behind methodological excuses. And while there may be some (considerable) merit to this approach, we do not feel that it is neces-sary to do so. Design limitations notwithstanding, our approach was sound, and our survey instrument reasonably credible. (See appendix A for a deeper discussion of our methodology.) So, what is going on?

On the one hand, the results speak for themselves: neither CIT training nor personal and professional relationships appear to have any impact on officer outcomes during MHCFS. That in itself is interesting and contrib-utes enormously to the limited research we currently possess on the topic of CIT (see chapter 3). More so, however, it is important to keep in mind exactly what a bivariate correlation is doing: it is teasing out the likeli-hood of a relationship between two variables by comparing the observed relationship with what we would expect given chance, alone. In this case, there is no observed difference between cadets and officers who had CIT training on the outcomes than those who did not have such training. All things equal, then, and on the surface, CIT does *not* matter, nor does per-sonal/professional relationships. This does not go very far in encouraging confidence in structural holes and our other theories discussed in the previ-ous chapter.

But what it does not do is tell us *why.* If there is not something unique about the officer, then is there something about the MHCFS itself that can help explain these apparent null findings? To more closely explore this ques-tion, we turn to our vignettes.

Table 4.3 Bivariate Results Pearson's Correlation for CIT and Volunteering for CIT

	CIT Training	Volunteered	Cadet/Officer	% Arrest	% Involuntary Commitment	% Informal Resolution	% Do Nothing
CIT Training	—	0.091*	0.361**	−0.012	0.023	−0.069	0.082*
Volunteered		—	0.101*	−0.046	0.103*	−0.055	−0.112**
Cadet/Officer			—	−0.176**	0.086*	−0.007	0.034
% Arrest				—	−0.428**	−0.286**	−0.048
% Involuntary Commitment					—	−0.667**	−0.233**
% Informal Resolution						—	0.116**
% Do Nothing							—

Note: Significant correlations flagged at the $p < 0.05$ with a *; significant correlations flagged at the $p < 0.01$ with a **.

Table 4.4   Bivariate Results Pearson's Correlation for Knowing a MH Professional and Having Family with MHDs

	Professional	Family	% Arrest	% Involuntary Commitment	% Informal Resolution	% Do Nothing
Professional	–	0.085*	–0.095*	0.040	0.052	–0.005
Family	–	–	–0.055	0.018	–0.002	0.053
% Arrest	–	–	–	–0.428**	–0.286**	–0.048
% Involuntary Commitment	–	–	–	–	–0.667**	–0.233**
% Informal Resolution	–	–	–	–	–	0.116**
% Do Nothing	–	–	–	–	–	–

Note: Significant correlations flagged at the $p < 0.05$ with a *; significant correlations flagged at the $p < 0.01$ with a **.

HYPOTHETICAL MHCFS SCENARIOS

There are very few ways to explore police officer decision-making, and each way has merit, but mostly shortcomings. It could reasonably be argued that the "best" way to observe police officer decision-making is to literally observe their behavior: presented with a given situation, *how* do police respond? The shortcoming to this approach should be obvious: observing behavior is not to observe decision-making. Rather, it is to determine the outcome of that decision-making process. To make conclusions about decision-making based on that processes' outcome is to put the cart before the horse, and to second guess the intentions and cognition of the law enforcement officer. So actual observation turns out not to be ideal.

One way to get past this is to have the police officer *explain* their decision-making process *after* observing their behavior. This approach certainly has merit: such a researcher would successfully get at the decision-making process in tandem with the actual impact of that process. This approach, too, suffers from several shortcomings, both methodologically and conceptually. Conceptually, it fails from the start to get at any implicit biases that affect the officer's decision-making (by "bias," we refer to the idea that subjectivity must *per force* enter into any decision-making process, be it that of police officers or an academic). This is so because much of our decision-making is influenced by unexamined biases of which we are unaware. While police are, indeed, trained to engage in deliberate decision-making, all officers will bring with them their own inherent biases, from the more crude racist and sexist biases to the more benign biases associated with an officer's demeanor and general disposition toward calls for service. Thus, by asking police to explain their decision-making process, we are putting an undue amount of trust in their capacity to be self-aware: a rather high standard that even scientists refuse to work under.

There is another problem associated with this approach at the level of method, namely: one could not stop the officer and ask them to explain their process as soon as it is resolved. Or, perhaps more accurately, one could not stop and ask the officer to explain their decision-making process immediately after the *initial* resolution of the MHCFS: the officer is still engaged in the call for service, be it with witnesses, service providers, report writing, crime scene establishment, *inter alia*. Indeed, the officer is *still making decisions* at this point. All this means that the officer would need to be interviewed about their decision-making process well after the event itself is resolved. Ironically, this would allow the officer to introspect a little too much, retrojecting intentions and processes that were not actually there in the moment. This would be even more likely because anyone in such a scenario would be likely to forget the details of the event. There are certainly methodological

answers to mitigate these concerns; we are not convinced, however, that they
do so sufficiently. More importantly, perhaps, is the fact that such methodological measures would indeed only *mediate* any threats to a study's internal
validity, not eliminate them completely.

Perhaps the weakest of all is simply asking police officers how they
respond to MHCFS. While a good starting place—and, indeed, represents
how we started in developing our scenarios—it is only that. Interviews and
focus groups in the context of this research question would result in super-
ficial and inflated findings more so, perhaps, than interviews after the fact.

At this point, it is likely that the reader is gearing up for us to provide a
strong justification for how we approached our research design, and a demon-
stration for why our chosen methodology is far superior to what has already
been described. On the contrary: we are well aware of the limitations of our
data gathering method. We simply suggest that while ours may be handi-
capped by serious methodological concerns, it is also the most cost- and time-
efficient while still getting to the heart of our research question. We employed
a multivariate vignette design that was able to control for several variables
randomly distributed within surveys and within vignettes (see appendix A for
a more detailed discussion of our vignette creation and appendix C for all of
the vignette presented to the officers). We then asked police and cadets how
likely they would be to respond to specific outcomes, namely, those already
discussed above: arrest, involuntary commitment, informal resolution, and
doing nothing.

The limitations of such an approach are pretty clear: we are presenting
officers with hypothetical situations and asking them to predict how they
will behave; from these results, we then try to predict why they would
behave the way they suggested. So, three problems become apparent. First,
even with more detailed variables, we still suffer from the problem of, basically, second-guessing our respondents. For example, if we uncover that
the gender of the hypothetical an individual with a MHD impacts an officer's decision outcome, net of controls, we are still assuming their process
included some aspect of gender. Although our statistical models may support
this assumption, it does remain an assumption. Second, it is exceptionally
well-established in psychology since at least the late 1950s with Festinger's
When Prophecy Fails was first published (but was recognized well before
then among philosophers and theologians, and anyone familiar with the
biblical books of Ecclesiastes or Romans or the teachings of the Buddha
is aware of) that people's behavior does not generally follow their beliefs
or attitudes, what is commonly called cognitive dissonance. Thus, though
our respondents may say they will do *x*, this in no way assures they will
not, in fact, do *y* when they are actually faced with the circumstances. This
is a common problem for anyone involved in social research and is best

understood as the methodological rivalry between attitudinal and behavioral measurements.

Third and finally, it bears pointing out that our scenarios *are* indeed hypothetical. We have done our level best to general realistic and likely scenarios for our respondents through the use of expert reviews and input (see appendices A and B), but it remains true that any success we have had in generating some realism is, in fact, simulated, that is, not real. So, we are not only left with the twin problems of the research second-guessing the police officer and the police officer second-guessing themselves, but we are also left with the conundrum of our vignettes second-guessing reality. It is at this point, perhaps, that studies exploring fewer compelling questions would raise their hands in defeat and move on to more methodologically facile questions. But the question of how do police respond to MHCFS and *why* is compelling enough that we are happily willing to cope with methodological stumbling blocks and their implications for the accuracy of our findings.

The empirical issues associated with vignettes are not that different from other approaches. Vignettes, however, have several characteristics that do, indeed, make them desirable. For example, we are able to manipulate our counterfactuals, rather than rely on the environment to do so (otherwise known as the "hope" approach to science, which should not be discouraged as so much of biological taxonomy relied on "informed luck" during the 1800s and early 1900s). In addition, we can get at their (albeit potential) decision-making process immediately, rather than waiting for a complete resolution of a situation when an officer may be free to sit and discuss their decisions in depth. Finally, as anyone who has ever collected data would know, regardless of the data gathering approach, surveys can be more efficient than literal observations, both in terms of time and money, and this should not be discounted in any researcher's decision-making process.

Appendix C describes the creation of our vignette universe in detail. We note here only that we were able to manipulate several vignette domains (randomly) within that universe: the crime type, the gender of the PwMI, the perceived PwMI's diagnosis, and the extent to which the PwMI was compliant to the officer's demands. Table 4.5 presents the details of these variables, as well as correlation coefficients at the first-order level.

It is not surprising that crime type did not influence officer decision-making in this context, in part because both crime types were not that serious, but also because it is often the case that crime type overrides officer discretion. Similarly, sex has no impact on the outcome. Perhaps this result can be explained as the police being hyper aware of the appropriateness of using gender in their decision-making. We would argue—and develop this

Table 4.5 Bivariate Results Pearson's Correlation for Vignette Variables (Level 1) and DVs

	Vig_Crime	Vig_Sex	Vig_Diagnosis	Vig_Compliance	% Arrest	%Involuntary Commitment	% Informal Resolution	% Do Nothing
Vig_Crime	—	−0.016	0.010	−0.005	−0.004	−0.011	0.051	−0.098**
Vig_Sex		—	−0.016	−0.016	0.014	0.007	−0.013	−0.045
Vig_Diagnosis			—	−0.026	−0.300**	0.478**	−0.250**	−0.063
Vig_Compliance				—	0.132**	0.080*	−0.206**	−0.073
% Arrest					—	−0.428**	−0.286**	−0.048
% Involuntary Commitment						—	−0.667**	−0.233**
% Informal Resolution							—	0.116**
% Do Nothing								—

Note: Significant correlations flagged at the $p < 0.05$ with a *; significant correlations flagged at the $p < 0.01$ with a **.

argument further in chapter 6—that it has more to do with the impact of sex simply being overridden by other concerns.

Those concerns, according to these data, are the perceived diagnosis of the individual with a MHD, and the level of their compliance. The latter finding is far from surprising to anyone who studies police, where suspect demeanor, after crime seriousness, tends to be the number one predictor of formal versus informal disposition. The coefficients for this variable are not striking, however. More striking are the coefficients associated with perceived diagnosis, which can be summed up thusly: arrest and informal resolutions are more likely if the perceived diagnosis is intoxication, and commitment is more likely if the perceived diagnosis is schizophrenia/depression. Admittedly, these outcomes are another example of science telling us something we already know. But they do more than that: they confirm what we hoped to have known: police are taking what could reasonably be considered appropriate action during MHCFS based on a host of *relevant* variables even more so than other variables that we know to predict police behavior.

These are encouraging results, but they are also first-order results. In chapter 6, we turn to more sophisticated multivariate models that will help us more fully flesh out the decision-making process of police officers during mental health calls for service.

Chapter 5

Police Training

A More Detailed Look

The picture painted from our initial zero- and first-order statistics is at once encouraging and somewhat deflating. On the one hand, it appears that police are doing what they should be doing in responding to MHCFS. But on the other hand, it appears that CIT is perhaps not making the difference one might otherwise want it to. In this chapter, we want to explore these first impressions in more detail but employing more sophisticated statistical models. In doing so, we are not making the claim that more sophisticated means more accurate. Indeed, although the mixed models we employ here provide more detail than those bivariate models in our preceding chapter, it is true that multivariate models can never tell us anything different than univariate and bivariate models, insofar as the former are really a function of the latter. Nevertheless, it is that detail that we are especially interested in, and it is mixed models that afford us such an opportunity.

In the previous chapter, we saw that CIT did not matter all that much in predicting dispositional outcomes, nor were type of crime or the gender of the civilian. Compliance and perceived diagnosis, however, did seem to have an impact, such that *arrest* and *informal resolutions* are more likely if the perceived diagnosis is intoxication, and commitment is more likely if the perceived diagnosis is schizophrenia/depression. In some respects, these findings are in line with what we know about predictors of police officer decision making. And even the perceived diagnosis findings make sense in context. The vignette approach of our survey, however, provides us with an even greater opportunity to dive into that context, by using mixed modeling.

Mixed models in statistics allow the analyst to explore their data in such a way that both slopes and intercepts can be "tailored" to design decisions and hypotheses. This was most appropriate for our particular data because of the nested nature of our vignettes. In preparing our models, we relied heavily on the work of Auspurg and Hinz (2016) and Luke (2011; see appendix A). This preparation involved a number of steps toward model building, the details of which can be found in Jachimowski (2018a). In the end, we settled on ten models exploring each potential outcome according to both level 1 and levels 1 and 2 variables.

What follows are tabular and narrative explanations of our findings, in light of our interest in what influences the decision making of officers. We do not provide all of our tables, or all the coefficients, but focus instead on what we believe to be the most interesting and compelling findings. This is not to "juke the stats"; the complete findings are publicly available elsewhere. Rather, it is the goal to focus on a discussion of the data as well as make a scholarly book that remains accessible.

To avoid making this section unnecessarily complicated, we only provide a brief description of how mixed models function. The analysis starts with a model which only contains level 2 variables as the fixed effects. Due to the use of the bottom-up method, the next step was creating models that continue to increase the model fit for the dependent variable. To create the best model fit, the -2 Loglikelihood was used to calculate a χ^2 to determine if the addition of the variable(s) significantly improved the model. Similar to other aspects of mixed models, there is no hard and fast rule as to the best way to calculate the change in model fit (Auspurg & Hinz, 2016; Luke, 2011). Researchers suggest using the Akaike Information Criterion (AIC) and Schwarz's Bayesian Information Criterion (BIC) to avoid error in model deviance due to the number of parameters in the model (Auspurg & Hinz, 2016; Luke, 2011). However, the AIC and BIC tests do not allow the researcher to determine if it is a statistically better model (Fields, 2017). Due to the lack of theoretical implications which could help build the models, the researcher used the -2 Loglikelihood in order to have a better grasp on the variables which are making a statistical difference in the models.

ARREST

There are four variables that indicated they created better fitting models for the level 2 variables (see table 5.1): *CIT* (-2LL = 6,130.408, $p < 0.01$), *CITVol* (-2LL = 4,796.674, $p < 0.01$), *CAD/POL* (-2LL = 4,792.815, $p < 0.05$), and *yearspolice* (-2LL = 4,132.770, $p < 0.01$). The χ^2 values continue to be statistically significant until adding demographic variables into the models. The column furthest to the right indicates if the variable was removed from the overall model before adding in the next term. In the case of the variable sex because there was not a statistically significant difference between the model which contained *CIT*, *CITVol*, *CAD/POL*, and

Table 5.1 Arrest Model Building 1—Level 2 Variables

Variable	−2 Loglikelihood	df	χ^2	Removed from model
Null Model	6,179.740	71	–	–
CIT	6,130.408	71	49.332**	no
CITVol	4,796.674	65	1,333.734**	no
CAD/POL	4,792.815	66	3.859*	no
Yearspolice	4,132.770	62	660.045**	no
Sex	4,132.050	63	0.72	yes
Race	4,131.133	63	1.637	yes
Area_Dummy	4,130.291	64	2.479	yes
Deptsize_Dummy	4,131.681	64	1.089	yes
Age_Dummy	4,127.756	66	5.014	yes

Note: Significant correlations flagged at the $p < 0.05$ with a *; significant correlations flagged at the $p < 0.01$ with a **.

yearspolice, the sex variable was removed before adding in the race variable. The best model which was created with only level 2 variables when assessing the likelihood of arrest had a −2LL of 4,132.700. These findings suggest that having CIT training, volunteering for that training, whether the respondent was a cadet or officer, and the years of service are important when evaluating variables which change the outcome of arrest, as well as a better model.

As we conclude our model building and analyze the final model (table 5.2), we found our models for *arrest* as a disposition fit the data reasonably well ($\chi^2 = 21.576$, $p < 0.05$). Of the variables that we ultimately introduced into the equation, only the variable measuring years as a police officer was statistically significant. The *estimate* coefficient (0.602) indicated that a police officer was more likely to employ arrest given any scenario *net of controls.*

Table 5.2 Arrest Model 4—Level 1 and Level 2 Variables

	−2 Loglikelihood	df	χ^2
Final Model ALL	4,133.082	105	21.576*
Variable	f-ratio	Estimate	T-ratio
Intercept		−35.796	−764
CIT	0.305	−8.147	−582
CITVol	0.102	0.948	0.320
Yearspolice	3.969*	0.602	1.992*
vig_diagnosis	90.179**	9.058	2.653
vig_compliance	11.645**	−8.878	−3.312
Interactions			
vig_crime*vig_sex	6.350*	3.216	0.952
vig_crime*vig_diagnosis*vig_sex	7.869*	−13.106	−1.932

Note: Significant correlations flagged at the $p < 0.05$ with a *; significant correlations flagged at the $p < 0.01$ with a **.

This finding itself is interesting and, quite frankly, counter to most policing research. Its uniqueness, however, maybe due to the fact that we are explicitly looking at scenarios involving PwMI rather than any generic or typical calls for service. More distressing for our purposes is the fact that neither CIT training nor volunteering for CIT training had any measurable effect on a police officer's disposition to affect an arrest. While the coefficient for CIT training was in the "correct" direction—that is, negative, such that receiving CIT training reduced the likelihood of arrest—it was far from any acceptable alpha level threshold ($t = |-0.552|$). We similarly note that this model failed to find any statistical significance with our interaction terms (the crime and the sex of the suspect, and the crime X sex X diagnosis). It is reasonable to assume that such null results are the product of our methodological limitations. Be this as it may, we accept them at face value, with the qualification that replication with more rigorous sampling methods may be employed.

INVOLUNTARY COMMITMENT

The next set of models focuses on the likelihood of the participant involuntarily committing the individual in the vignette. As with the arrest dependent variable models, table 5.3 each represents individual models as the researcher continued to include only relevant variables, one at a time. To begin, there are three variables which made statistically significant differences when added to the model. With the inclusion of the *CIT* variable only (no random effects) the $-2LL$ of 3,762.757 indicated there was a difference between whether officers or cadet were likely to involuntarily commit an individual based on their training, preliminarily ($x^2 = 28.623$, $p < 0.01$). The *CITVol* variable provided the most significant change in the overall $-2LL$ ($\chi^2 = 685.537$, $p < 0.01$),

Table 5.3   IC Model Building 1—Level 2 Variables

Variable	−2 Loglikelihood	df	χ2	Removed from model
Null Model	6,641.030	71	–	–
CIT	3,762.757	72	28.623**	no
CITVol	3,077.220	65	685.537**	no
CAD/POL	3,076.857	66	0.363	yes
Yearspolice_mc	2,629.103	62	448.117**	no
Sex	2,630.073	63	−0.97	yes
Race	2,630.132	63	−1.029	yes
Area_Dummy	2,629.448	64	−0.345	yes
Deptsize_Dummy	2,631.776	64	−2.673	yes
Age_Dummy	2,629.663	66	−0.56	yes

Note: Significant correlations flagged at the $p < 0.05$ with a *; significant correlations flagged at the $p < 0.01$ with a **.

Table 5.4   IC Model 4—Level 1 and Level 2 Variables

Final Model ALL	−2 Loglikelihood 4,516.081	df 105	χ2 0.356
Variable	f-ratio	Estimate	T-ratio
CIT	0.000	0.315	0.015
CITVol	0.709	−3.604	−0.824
vig_diagnosis	458.776**	−14.327	−3.172*
vig_compliance	18.949**	−5.713	−1.555
Interactions			
vig_diagnosis*vig_crime	17.074**	–	–
vig_diagnosis*vig_sex*vig_compliance	4.839*	16.627	1.805

Note: Significant correlations flagged at the $p < 0.05$ with a *; significant correlations flagged at the $p < 0.01$ with a **.

and the *yearspolice* variable had a χ^2 of 448.117 ($p < 0.01$). Unlike the arrest variable, the *CAD/POL* variable did not indicate a statistically significant difference when added to the model building. The smallest −2LL produced by these significant variables was 2,629.103.

Police are generally reluctant to invoke involuntary commitment unless absolutely necessary. Understanding why police do choose such an option is especially important, therefore. In our case, the models for involuntary commitment largely mirror those for arrest, insofar as CIT training and volunteering for CIT training had no effect. In addition, while volunteering for training was in the "correct" direction (namely, negative), that for CIT itself was in the "wrong" direction (namely, positive). However, the latter was so small, and its accompanying *t* value so small, as to literally, and not just statistically, best be understood as equaling a zero-effect size. The only variable to retain any statistically significant relationship with involuntary commitment was diagnosis: if a suspect appeared to suffer from a SMI, rather than mere intoxication, the likelihood of involuntary commitment disturbingly *went down*. This coefficient was not insubstantial (*estimate* = −14.327, $p < 0.01$), and deserves considerable scrutiny (see table 5.4).

INFORMAL RESOLUTION

The third dependent variable analyzed for our CIT research focus is the likelihood of the respondent engaging in some type of *informal resolution* at the scene. Like the other dependent variables, each term was added to the overall model individually and only variables which created statistically significant better models were kept in the model (see table 5.5). Similar to the *involuntary commitment* models, there are three variables which created a statistically better model, *CIT*, *CITVol*, and *yearspolice*. Also similar to the

Table 5.5   IR Model Building 1—Level 2 Variables

Variable	−2 Loglikelihood	df	$\chi2$	Removed from model
Null Model	6,641.030	71	–	–
CIT	6,586.779	72	54.25**	no
CITVol	5,239.864	65	1,346.915**	no
CAD/POL	5,237.801	66	2.0263	yes
Yearspolice_mc	4,540.730	62	699.134**	no
Sex	4,540.432	63	0.298	yes
Race	4,540.867	63	−0.137	yes
Area_Dummy	4,536.393	64	3.791	yes
Deptsize_Dummy	4,536.463	66	0.476	yes
Age_Dummy	4,536.400	68	0.539	yes

Note: Significant correlations flagged at the $p < 0.05$ with a *; significant correlations flagged at the $p < 0.01$ with a **.

third arrest model (see table 5.2) and the third involuntary commitment model (see table 5.4), *CITVol* had the largest impact on creating a better model with a $\chi2 = 1,346.915$ ($p < 0.01$), while *yearspolice* had the second largest $\chi2$ of 699.134 ($p < 0.01$). Finally, whether or not the respondent said they had ever had CIT training had the lowest effect on the likelihood of an informal resolution ($\chi2 = 54.25$, $p < 0.01$).

The likelihood of the police employing an informal resolution during a MHCFS, as with both arrest and involuntary commitment, completely unaffected by CIT training or volunteering for such training. Unsurprisingly, the demeanor (compliant or not) of the suspect *did* inform an officer's choice, specifically: officers were more likely to informally resolve a MHCFS than not *if* the suspect was perceived as being compliant with an officer's demands. The effect size for this variable was not insubstantial (*estimate* = 15.107, $p < 0.01$), but, as we indicated, is not exactly surprising (see table 5.6). Just as the police are more likely to informally resolve any call for service if the suspect is compliant, so too is it just as reasonable to assume that an officer would find a suspect's mental health "strong enough" to justify "letting them off, easy." Perhaps more interesting was the statistically significant and considerable effect of the interaction of diagnosis and compliance on informal resolution (*estimate* = 8.112, $p < 0.05$). Basically, compliant suspects with perceivable symptoms of schizophrenia were *more* likely to be at the receiving end of an informal resolution. This is fascinating, and perhaps suggests the hesitancy of the police to involve themselves with the mental health system when the individual in question is perceived as mentally fit enough to comply, despite exhibiting serious symptoms of SMI, as compared to something police are more familiar with, namely public intoxication. While this

Table 5.6 IR Model 4—Level 1 and Level 2 Variables

Final Model ALL	−2 Loglikelihood 4,268.311	df 105	chi2 98.054**
Variable	f-ratio	Estimate	T-ratio
CIT	0.112	7.048	0.335
CITVol	0.004	−0.265	−0.061
vig_crime	5.756*	−5.196	−1.402
vig_diagnosis	24.256**	4.51	1.140
vig_compliance	36.162**	15.107	3.956*
Interactions			
vig_diagnosis*vig_compliance	8.112*	10.306	1.857

Note: Significant correlations flagged at the $p < 0.05$ with a *; significant correlations flagged at the $p < 0.01$ with a **.

finding is somewhat beyond the purview of our book, it nonetheless requires further comment, which we undertake in chapter 6.

Do Nothing

So, we now come to the final disposition with which officers could respond to each scenario: *doing nothing*. As table 5.7 demonstrates, nothing remained statistically significant in the final model. As we see it, there are two reasonable explanations for this result, one of which is related to our survey methodology, the other of which is based on the reality of policing. First: methodologically, it could simply be the case that officers were not disposed to answer, "do nothing." Given the controlled environment of survey administration, the time allotted to them to consider the situation may have encouraged them to "do something," despite *do nothing* being a reasonable response. Additionally, the very phrase "do nothing" may have been off-putting. After all, even if an officer were to release a PwMI into the custody of their caretaker, they have certainly *not* done nothing: they have interacted with civilians and maintained/restored order. That is certainly something.

Table 5.7 Do Nothing Model 4—Level 1 and Level 2 Variables

Final Model ALL	−2 Loglikelihood 2,733.730	df 105	$\chi 2$ 94.004**
Variable	f-ratio	Estimate	T-ratio
Intercept		0.381	0.026
CIT	0.015	−0.578	−0.124
CITVol	0.529	0.712	0.727

Note: Significant correlations flagged at the $p < 0.05$ with a *; significant correlations flagged at the $p < 0.01$ with a **.

Second: it could simply be that the police are indeed indisposed to do nothing in any scenario involving PwMI. They may, indeed, see their situation either as a serious enough threat to the public or themselves or as an opportunity for compassion. In either case, *doing nothing* would simply not be an option. We are, of course, indulging ourselves in speculation at this point, but we believe that this null finding is the result of some unknown combination of both possibilities: our respondents felt compelled to not *do nothing*, both because of the controlled nature of survey administration and because they themselves would want to do something.

SUMMARY THOUGHTS

What are we to make of these somewhat deflating results? Perhaps a better way to ask the question is this: what sort of picture do these results paint about the police? In short, a rather good one, as far as we are concerned, even if the actual impact of CIT is value-laden or even existent. To begin, it is noteworthy that whether its CIT training itself, or specifically volunteering for such training, the effect (or lack thereof) was essentially the same. This is telling and paints a picture familiar to those who work with court-mandated treatment for drug users: it does not matter whether someone wants the treatment or not, *getting* the treatment is what matters. So, too, apparently, with CIT: whether the training is undertaken as part of regular in-service, or whether it is taken voluntarily seems to have no effect on its impact. The training is enough to have an effect. (Incidentally, while there are problems with our sampling strategy, this speaks to its validity insofar as it eliminates those who would self-select into a CIT program.)

To put it plainly, CIT and CIT training (along with a host of other theoretically reasonable variables) did not appear to matter for our models. The utility of our book may therefore be questioned by close readers. After all, of what value is a book predicated on a conclusion that could go something like this, "special training to help officers respond appropriately to mental health calls for service does not seem to actually affect how police would hypothetically respond to such calls?" As we wrote at the start of this summary section, we believe that this finding actually speaks volumes about the police, their interactions with individuals who have a MHD specifically, and their interactions with the public more generally. Basically: the police are doing what they are supposed to be doing and doing it well.

Here is what we mean by this statement. The relationship between the police and society in the United States is both philosophically and literally confrontational. As numerous policing scholars have noted since the 1950s, policing in a democracy is, by its nature, a paradox. (Perhaps the government's report *The Challenge of Crime in a Free Society* should have been more aptly titled *The Challenge of Police in a Free Society*, after all). While America is a republic, it is a country that espouses democratic ideals, which include a *host* of freedoms. But the very purpose of the police is to *deny* liberty. Indeed, the majority of the corpus (and penumbra) of the U.S. Constitution dictates how the government—especially the police—can go about doing just that: denying civilians their otherwise inalienable rights and liberties.

In addition, the history of policing in the United States can be understood as one of, first, government suppression of specific minority populations (African American slaves in the South; Jim Crow throughout the United States; Catholics in the Northeast; *inter alia*). Combined with the inherit confrontational nature of the police, it is no wonder why, during the early 1990s riots sparked by the Rodney King beating, people harkened back to the 1960s "long hot summers," or why in the series of riots against the police in the second decade of the twentieth century, people were comparing the situation to the early 1990s or, again, to the 1960s. This in tandem with perpetual individual or detail level examples of harassment, abuse of power, excessive force, and corruption have created a mythos surrounding the police as being anything but the angelic army lead by St. Michael.

Everything we stated in the last two paragraphs is an accurate description of policing and the police. But it is only a part of the picture—and a part we suggest that is most often described by the media and within classrooms. But for the majority of police–civilian interactions, both parties walk away without any hurt feelings or hurt bodies. Most people still call the police—not when there is a crime, but when there is any sort of perceived problem or even the whiff of suspicion. In one of the author's hometown (in rural Wyoming), the police are frequently called on to chase moose from downtown when they wander in. And when the police are called to such cases, they are clearly acting in such a way that upholds the honor and integrity expected of their rank and position in the majority of cases. Perhaps the logic here is tautological, but it holds: why else would individuals continue to call the police for help in matters that are both mundane and dangerously serious?

One could answer by pointing out that there are no other options. We do not believe this is true, as there are many other options (churches, community leaders, whether licit or illicit). Even if it were true, however, it is also true that, across race/ethnicity, sex/gender, and various levels of socioeconomic status/disadvantage, the majority of civilians *like* the police (or approve of them, or believe them to be good people, and so on, according to the surveyor's preference). Further, this is a finding that has remained stable across time, too. This can be validated by looking through any number of studies about public perceptions of the police found at website for the National

Criminal Justice Reference Service (NCRS). As just one example, we quote from Miller and colleagues' 2004 report to the Department of Justice:

> Citizens' opinions of the police are positive and quite stable over time—at least in the absence of significant shifts in police policy or media scandals. The same is true of levels of consumer satisfaction among those who have had voluntary encounters with the police. This stability exists even in the face of some notable variation in news coverage of the police.

In pointing this out, we are not condoning police violence, abuse of force, corruption, etc. Rather, we are pointing out that even in the face of such negative behavior, the police generally and consistently are (at least viewed as) doing their job and doing it well. Thus, our results may simply reflect this: with or without CIT training, police are not only likely to behave similarly in response to MHCFS but do so in ways that appear commensurate with best practices.

This having been discussed, we now consider what this means for our theoretical underpinnings, which we originally established in chapter 4. Additionally, in the following chapter we take up the questions of policy implications and future research.

Chapter 6

Moving Forward

Theory and Practice

In this concluding chapter, we fully consider our findings in light of three specific topics: theory, practice, and future research. These three topics are, of course, related to each other. Because of this, there will likely be some overlap in our proceeding discussion. We do our best, however, to isolate each topic so that we can clearly discuss each in terms of how our study contributes to the corpus of literature in each domain.

THEORY

At the end of chapter 3, we proposed three theories that, while not being explicitly tested in our study, nevertheless informed our research process: the theory of interpersonal relations (TIR); structural holes and weak ties; and systems theory. To briefly recapitulate our outline of their tenets:

- *TIR*: The nature of the relationship between client and provider is intimate and surpasses pecuniary concerns. These intimate ties must be considered when understanding the relationship and its outcome.
- *Structural holes/weak ties*: It is not how many people (or organizations) a person (or organization) knows that matters; it is who they know in terms of the social capital they bring to bear, along with their own social network.
- *Systems theory*: Social systems, such as criminal justice and mental health, are intimately connected with one another insofar as what one does will affect the others.

Our findings, again, do not test these theories; but just as they informed our understanding of how CIT was important, so too do we believe our findings can endogenously inform the underpinnings of each theory.

Peplau's TIR

By its nature, policing is not inherently a commodified process. This is not to deny that financial concerns do not inhere themselves in policing; they most certainly do. Rather, it is to suggest that on the street, line officers are not immediately concerned with a department's financial well-being. Certainly, this may enter into their equation, but not with the sort of weight that it would a CEO of a large firm, or even the owner of a small business. It is largely because of this characteristic of policing that DiIulio in 1995 stated that policing, like most public services, employs nonoperational goals—that is, goals where the ability to compare how the organization was *before* to *now* cannot be enumerated or, at the very least, cannot be accomplished objectively and with any semblance of clear reasoning.

This is true of policing in large part because arrest is not itself tied directly to the outcome in question, namely criminal behavior. While most laypersons and politicians would assume that such a connection exists (as would the police during the so-called professional era of policing; cf. Cooper, 2015), there are at least three things that conspire to prevent this association. First is the reactive nature of policing: if the goal is to prevent crime, then policing constitutionally has no business doing so. With very few and difficultly obtained exceptions (collectively known as inchoate crimes), a crime *must have been committed* before police can, in fact, do something. But what if one argues that prevention is not the goal, and that, rather, crime can be prevented via apprehension? The logic of this argument is that by removing offenders, we can reduce crime. While this is logical, it fails empirically: as scholars have known since at least 1979 (see Cohen and Felson's initial articulation of routine activities theory), and as police have known for far longer, *everyone* is capable of committing crime. Effectively, this means that removing offenders does nothing to reduce crime, because a pool of motivated offenders remains at large (again, see Cohen & Felson, 1979).

Finally, the third reason that policing is nonoperational is, in part, because the crime rate is not, in fact, the only or even perhaps the main thing when people think of what they want from the police. Rather, they want quick or at least predictable response times; friendly and professional police officers who are also approachable; and they want to feel safe in their neighborhood, which has less to do with crime, *per se*, and more to do with the amount and character of police presence. And all of these things are clearly categorical in nature: there is no nonarbitrary numerical way to measure "feeling safe" or "satisfaction with the police" as there is to measure the crime rate. Thus, what police do is by and large and reasonably *nonoperational.*

This observation is important for understanding how TIR applies to the police in terms of MHCFS generally and our study specifically. Essentially, when police respond to MCHS, they are involved in more than a financial transaction. Rather, they are involved in a human moment. Police are trained for this sort of thing, regardless of the type of call. As anyone who has walked away from a traffic ticket feeling good can attest, police can be very "human" in how they do their job. Thus, as TIR can guide nurses in assisting their patients, so too can TIR guide police in their interactions with PwMI. We expand this statement in more detail below when we discuss policy implications. Here, though, it suffices to simply suggest that policing is a human service, and as such can benefit from any theory that guides civilian encounters. And we saw from our results, police are doing more with individuals with MHDs than just arresting them: they are just as likely to involuntarily commit them or refer them to the appropriate agency. In short, police do not treat the world as nails and act themselves as hammers: rather, they look at the problem at hand and choose whichever tool is most likely to not just help, but to help with compassion.

Structural Holes/Weak Ties

According to this theory, if officers have a loose network composed of key actors in the mental health field, they should be more likely to employ nonpunitive dispositions. As our models have it, however, this was not the case. Simply stated: knowing people in the field, or even knowing PwMI in their personal life, did not really matter; this was a very surprising finding. Structural holes and weak ties have ample support in the literature. Granted, the majority of this literature concerns financially motivated institutions, but such research does exist for the public sector, as well, including the police (cf. Cooper, 2015). In addition, these relationships did show up in our zero- and first-order relationships but disappeared once we introduced multivariate models. Finally, it is often the case that professional matters do not take on special significance for someone until they become a personal matter (e.g., politicians or church leaders who are against same-sex marriage until a son or a daughter admits to having a same-sex partner). Why, then, would such relationships *not* affect an officer's decisions?

For the sake of speculation, let us accept that this is a real finding, in the sense of Types I and II error, in probabilistic statistics. We may be seeing the remnants of a professional era policing ethos. The professional era is broadly understood to span the late 1800s to about the mid-1970s (see Cooper, 2015 for a more detailed explication of policing during this time frame). One of the characteristics of this era was the generation of a sense that police were *the* professional crime fighters of America: that crime control, prevention, suppression, and, most importantly, *fighting* was the special purview of the police. All other actors—be they criminals, witnesses, civilians, or other public servants, including those involved in the mental health system—became at best witnesses, at worst offenders, but most often nuisances. It is possible that our finding that an officer's network and personal connections to mental health illnesses had no effect on their decision-making process during MHCFS was due in part to this professional era ethos yet lingering among the police.

We emphasize that we are engaging in educated speculation here, but it is nevertheless worth considering. If this is what we see going on, then it somewhat tampers the positive picture we have been painting about the police "doing their job with compassion." *Doing their job with compassion* and *being* the *professional crime fighter*—and all that both of those statements carry with them—are not, of course, logically mutually exclusive. But if we have learned anything from the professional era, it is that they are *practically* mutually exclusive. So, if such an antimony exists, then each principle at work must *perforce* tamper the other.

Systems Theory

Much of what we have said regarding structural holes/weak ties applies to systems theory, as well. We want to focus our comments here, though, on one particular finding: that police were more likely to involuntarily commit someone displaying signs of depression than someone displaying signs of schizophrenia. Again, we can only speculate as to what this means, but it is certainly an unanticipated finding. One would expect that the more serious the mental illness, the more serious consequence (in this case, involuntary commitment as opposed to informal resolution or doing nothing). This could represent a misunderstanding of the nature of schizophrenia. It could also represent a belief that depression can lead to suicide. This belief would likely be based on having more exposure to depression than schizophrenia in pop psychology. Regardless, it points to the need to increase training in the nature and consequences of all mental illnesses.

There is also likely an element of how the police are trained at work here. Namely: police are trained, among other things, to prevent immediate harm to themselves, to the public, and to the person of interest. Thus why, if depression is associated with self-harm, police are likely to employ involuntary commitment? More so, if police believe someone with a major mental illness is more likely to be already undergoing treatment, as opposed to depression which has a popular image of quiet suffering and self-medicating, especially with alcohol, they may be more likely to provide informal resolutions rather than invoke either the criminal justice or the mental health system. In either case, it's unclear whether the mental health system enters the decision-making process of the police *except* as a potential option among any that they can employ with discretion that is guided by their police training and experience rather than with any mental health training.

PRACTICE

Historically, police have framed individuals with MHDs as being extra-dangerous and unpredictable and have responded to MHCFS accordingly. In fairness to the police, this framework is reinforced and informed largely by society's own views regarding mental illness. Consequently, police will typically respond to MHCFS with an eye toward community protection at the expense of the PwMI's well-being. Arguably, this is a reasonable reaction—and a legally correct one. Nevertheless, just as there are occasions when arrest or involuntary commitment is certainly the right response to MHCFS, so too must there be MHCFS where the correct action is something less invasive, and where a measured response on the part of the police can preserve both the safety of the community and the well-being of the PwMI suspect.

With this as a background, we believe that at least three policy implications can be reasonably drawn from our research. First: while CIT and volunteering for CIT did not appear to matter in our final models, we did find these variables statistically significant at the individual level. While we do not deny our ultimate nonsignificant findings, our use of mixed models will, of course, impact our final statistical conclusions. In other words, we are not wholly convinced that our final models' findings in any way negate the idiosyncratic impact of CIT on the individual officer. In using mixed models, we risk falling into both the ecological and the component fallacies. We do not believe we have done so, and we stand by our final models, but this does not deny that there are going to be processes at work that we were unable to fully capture or understand. We tentatively believe that this is the case with CIT. Either, as we argued above, police are "doing their job" independently of CIT, or CIT does, on an individual level, impact their dispositional behavior. We lean this way because of prior research that suggests that this is, indeed, the case (Compton, Broussard, Reed, Crisafio, & Watson, 2015; Morabito et al., 2010). Policy makers and police administrators should, therefore, continue to consider and scrutinize CIT.

Second, although the models we discussed in chapter 5 failed to reach significance across a host of variables, at the individual level, we note that the presence of outpatient treatment facilities did, in fact, reduce the likelihood of arrest *and* involuntary commitment. This corroborates previous research (Constatine et al., 2010; Ringhoff, Rapp, & Robst, 2012). So, while it is fair to say that at one level, the presence of such facilities does not matter, at another level, they do. This should, therefore, be explored by policy makers as a viable community health and safety resources. Finally, while our final models did not distinguish between CIT and volunteering for CIT, the fact is that the willingness of officers to voluntarily acquire CIT consistently improved model fit, net of controls. This also jives well with prior research, which indicates that officers are looking for training to meaningful de-escalate encounters with PwMI (Lord & Bjerregaard, 2014). Policy makers should therefore consider having different levels of CIT training: requisite and voluntary.

FUTURE RESEARCH

We have already hinted at several avenues of research that we believe will be especially fruitful. In this section, we want to expand on these and offer what we think are the most promising areas of research in this domain.

In terms of methodological improvements, there are some very obvious ways to develop our methodology (see appendix A). Most of which are standard fare for social science, frankly: better, more randomized sample (a difficult but not impossible thing to achieve when studying the police). For example, a more random sample would bolster our external validity, and a larger sample would improve our power. Our power was sufficient for our models, but when employing mixed models with complex interaction terms, power remains an important concern, especially since, by and large, we were unable to find statistically significant variables. But of more interest to us has to do with our vignettes. We would be interested in seeing more complex vignettes that are also more representative of what police are likely to encounter. Although we did use several experts in developing our vignettes, we believe that more detailed vignettes could be constructed. Such vignettes would also explore more domains and factors.

Similarly, we would like to propose an alternative to the use of survey vignettes: using applied theater in conjunction with surveys, focus groups, interviews, *inter alia.* Studying officer behavior is inherently difficult in large part because the researcher is simply unable to truly manipulate the "treatment," as any undergraduate criminology methods students, fresh off of studying the Kansas City Preventive Patrol Experiment, can attest. We believe that one way to get closer to how officers would actually behave, rather than only being able to observe how they would plan on behaving (or getting lucky on a ride-along), would be having officers participate with actors in simulated MHCFS. Doing so would have the benefit of being able to manipulate the "treatment" variable(s), in addition to observing officer behavior in real time. In addition, it is an exercise that police are familiar with from both the academy and in-service, namely, routine training that employ simulations.

In the preceding paragraphs, we have already suggested several empirical avenues for future research. For example, further and more in-depth studies should be conducted exploring voluntary versus involuntary CIT at both the process and outcome stages. Additionally, studies should explore how the police perceive their role vis-à-vis PwMI and if CIT *really* changes that perception. Although we have argued that police tend to mirror society's perceptions of individuals with a MHD, we believe this is a reasonable argument; the fact is that research has not fully explored this. So, perhaps one of the reasons that we find so little statistically significant results in our study has to do with police truly not looking at PwMI all that differently compared to other suspects, common belief notwithstanding. After all, this would not be the first time the public or the police believed one thing about the police only to see that it simply was not true (a number of classic examples come to mind from social science research in the 1960s and 1970s; as just one example, the finding that detectives actually played very little role in solving crimes; cf. Cooper, 2015 for an overview of the research on policing in this decade). Ultimately, police and PwMI remain a very, very understudied and therefore not understood relationship that deserves the attention of social scientists.

FINAL REMARKS

We hope that we have established the importance of continuing to understand how police respond to mental health calls for service. In doing so, we further hope that research in this domain will continue at the level of both basic and applied science. We admit that our findings are very much inconclusive. If anything, however, these results only drive home the need for more research. Because police interactions with people with mental illnesses remain an exigent reality for law enforcement, providing both adequate resources and training—and more importantly the *correct* and *effective* resources and training—is imperative. This book, we hope, will provide a starting point for such future research endeavors.

Appendix A

How We Gathered Our Data

Although we feel that our book speaks to "more than" a single research project, or even an agenda, it remains true that about a third of our volume relies on data that we collected. While we did not want to distract from the main narrative of our text, we felt it necessary to discuss our methodology here in an appendix. In what follows, we describe our sampling process; our survey instrument; and how we approached our data once collected.

SAMPLING PROCEDURE

To inform the underlying thesis of our book, we conducted a cross-sectional study where we sampled both duly sworn law enforcement officers and police academy cadets. While many, if not most, social scientists may object to such a cross-sectional design, we note that most methodologists agree that quasi-experimental research designs are not only reasonable but often desired in the social sciences (for an extended discussion, we refer the reader to Bachman & Schutt, 2010; Muijs, 2011). As indicated above, our sample consisted of both sworn officers and academy cadets. In either case, we developed our sampling frame through convenience, ultimately generating one pool of subjects from several Pennsylvania police academies, and a second pool of police departments located in the following states: Pennsylvania, Delaware, Rhode Island, and Wyoming. As with employing a nonexperimental design, many social scientists may balk at our use of convenience sampling. While admitting the inherent limitations of such sampling (cf. Farrokhi & Mahmoudi-Hamidabad, 2012), particularly as applied to external validity, we nonetheless are not concerned about its implications for our subject matter, insofar as police are, by and large, a very homogenous sociopolitical organization (see the arguments developed thereto by Cooper, White, Ward, Raganella, & Saunders, 2014). Additionally, police and police departments are a notoriously difficult milieu to gather representative samples by using random sampling methodologies (BJS, 2016; Raganella & White, 2004). Ultimately, we believe this methodology meets two of the three of Ferber's (1977) criteria for analytic research: the population under examination, regardless of sampling strategy, is relevant to the research question; and given the standardized nature of policing in America since the mid-twentieth century (cf. Cooper, 2015), especially as concerning CIT, the third criterion of representativeness is at least approximated, if not met. It did not, however, meet Ferber's criterion concerning representativeness given the survey response rate.

In the end, we generated an $n = 118$ law enforcement officers and $n = 27$ police cadets. Given $a = 0.05$, $\beta = 0.80$, and $\rho^2 = 0.43$ (a roughly moderate to large effect size at the individual level of analysis), we would require $N = 62$ under the linear model. Given the vignette nature of our data (explained below), our sample size is necessarily increased factorially. Specifically, given a vignette universe of 24, and the exposure of 5 vignettes per survey with 6 vignette sets, each with a necessary $n = 62$, we would have required an actual $N = 315$ (for a discussion of power and vignette surveys, see Atzmuller & Steiner, 2010; Auspurg & Hinz, 2016). We distributed over 340 surveys, but did not meet the requisite 315 response rate. To this end, we acknowledge concern with the external validity of the models underpinning our discussion throughout the book. However, in addition to the homogeneous nature of police and policing, we also agree with Auspurg and Hinz (2016) that *internal validity* trumps external validity. What this means practically for our study is that while we could have increased statistical power by reducing the vignette exposure, to do so would have inherently limited our internal validity. Therefore, relying on what may be termed the "assumption of homogeneity" of police departments, we opt for the risk of theoretical precision over sampling representativeness.

SURVEY DEVELOPMENT

The actual survey instrument we used is included under appendix B. We wanted to include a brief discussion of our approach here, however, to clarify any questions about the analytic strategy we adopted and the choices that guided our data management, described below. We note at the outset that there is no gold standard for the type of survey we were interested in administering; therefore, our survey construction was guided by both the extant literature and the expert review of criminal justice actors (e.g., directors of police academies and police administrators). Additionally, we administered pretests and adjusted our survey accordingly, in addition to checking for criterion validity and other psychometric concerns. Our survey, of course, suffers from the standard methodological concerns, but in the end we found that its validity and reliability were robust and dependable. Finally, we note that we administered our surveys through the Internet and through the mail according to the preference of the respondents.

In addition to single response items (see appendix B), we included a number of factorial vignettes (FS), which were largely the focus of our survey. We adopted a vignette approach in order to simulate real-life scenarios that a police officer would reasonably be faced with. This survey construction method was particularly suited to our study because FS allow for just how complex police interactions with PwMI can become. Our FS construction was guided by Auspurg and Hinz (2016), and resulted in a multifactorial design of three dimensions at four levels and three dimensions at two levels (i.e., $4^2 3^1$), resulting in a total universe of twenty-four vignettes. These vignettes were distributed as equally as possible across each survey, with each respondent being exposed to five randomly selected vignettes. For a complete discussion of the survey methodology, see Jachimowski (2018a, chapters three and four).

VARIABLE INFORMATION

Table A.1

Variable	Survey Question or Measurement
Sex	What is your sex?
Race	Which of the following racial or ethnic group do you most closely identify? *Check all that apply.*
Race combined	Race was combined to include only white and non-white individuals.
Age	In years, how old will you be at the conclusion of this year?
Role	Officers and cadets were controlled by cadet being surveyed in-person.
Patrol area	Think of the place you patrol most frequently, how would you categorize that area?
Department size	How would you classify the size of your department?
Negative experience	Have you ever had a negative experience while trying to involuntarily commit an individual?
Cadet weeks	How many weeks have you been attending courses at the Criminal Justice Training Center?

Table A.1   (Continued)

Variable	Survey Question or Measurement
Years police	How many years have you been a sworn police officer? If less than one year, please indicate that.
CIT training	Have you ever received any type of *mental health* or *crisis intervention training?* If yes, go to the next question, if no, skip the next question.
Volunteered	Did you volunteer for the *mental health* or *crisis intervention training?*
Professional	Do you know someone professionally whom you can contact for questions on mental health, or if you need help during a call for service?
Family	Do you know someone with a serious mental illness, such as schizophrenia, bi-polar/manic, or major depressive disorder?
Resource type	Using SAMHSA—what types of resources were available in the officer's (or cadets) geographical location?
Resources	Total number of resources in the SAMHSA Directory
vig_sex	Within the vignettes, what was the person's (not officer) sex?
vig_diagnosis	Within the vignettes, what was the person's (not officer) symptoms of potential diagnosis?
vig_crime	Within the vignettes, what was the person's (not officer) behavior of potential crime?
vig_compliance	Within the vignettes, was the person (not officer) compliant with officer's demands/orders?

DATA MANAGEMENT AND ANALYSIS

Given the factorial nature of our surveys, we employed mixed models with both fixed and random effects. Preliminary first-order correlation matrices suggested potential multicollinearity between a small number of variables. First, two variables, "urban" and "suburban," were correlated above the traditionally adopted 0.70 correlation threshold ($r = -0.755, p < 0.05$); this was not born out in the variance inflation factors, however, which did not reach about 2.33. Further, there was unity between "depression" and "schizophrenia." Because of this, we collapsed these two variables into a single measurement which was measured as 0 = intoxicated and 1 = depression *or* schizophrenia. This is not ideal, given the distinction between these two diagnoses, but it was a statistical necessity. Otherwise, after running appropriate diagnostics, we did not identify any other risks to the Gauss Markov assumptions.

Appendix B

Survey Instruments

PRETEST SURVEY

Thank you for volunteering to pretest the following survey on police response to mental health calls for service. Due to your expertise in this area, I am very interested in any comments you have regarding the wording, the scenarios, or in general; for example, the survey layout, or missing information which may be important to get a complete understanding of the response. While taking the survey, please time how long it takes to complete the survey in its entirety. Note: Your answers will not be used in any research—after reading your feedback the survey will be discarded. Upon completion, contact me and I can make arrangements for it to be picked up. If you have any questions, please feel free to contact me at XX.

SECTION 1

Instructions: Please read each of the following scenarios. After you will be asked to answer questions about how you would respond to each situation as described in the scenario. There are no right or wrong answers.
  Example: After a long week at work, Nicole and some colleagues decide to go out and have a drink at a local bar. Nicole works as a veterinary technician and has had to make tough decisions regarding the health of an animal. Using the following scale, how likely do you feel it is that Nicole would get each one of the following alcoholic drinks?

0%		10%	20%	30%		40%	50%	60%	70%	80%	90%		100%	
No Chance		Low Chance		Some Chance			Good Chance			High Chance			Completely Certain	

Chance of Nicole ordering hard liquor, straight: ___
Chance of Nicole ordering hard liquor with a mixer: ___
Chance of Nicole ordering a beer or hard cider: ___
Chance of Nicole ordering another category of drink not listed: ___

Begin Answering the Following Survey Questions

1. While you are on patrol you receive a call for service, the dispatcher relays that the caller indicated the individual has a mental illness. According to the caller, the individual is asking for money from pedestrians and threatening suicide. When you arrive on the scene you identify as a police officer and the male is unresponsive of your commands. Using the following scale, how likely are you to do each of the following actions?

0%		10%	20%	30%	40%	50%	60%	70%		80%	90%		100%	
No Chance		Low Chance		Some Chance		Good Chance				High Chance			Completely Certain	

Likelihood of arresting the person and transport them to your holding facility: _____

Likelihood of arresting the person and seek to have them involuntarily committed: ____

Likelihood of an informal resolution at the scene (i.e., conflict resolution, warning): ____

Likelihood of doing nothing and leaving the scene: _____

2. While you are on patrol you receive a call for service, the dispatcher relays that the caller indicated the individual has a mental illness. According to the caller, the individual is acting strange and arguing with objects, they appear to be hallucinating. When you arrive on the scene you identify as a police officer and the male is responsive to your commands. Using the following scale, how likely are you to do each of the following actions?

0%		10%	20%	30%		40%	50%	60%	70%		80%	90%		100%	
No Chance		Low Chance		Some Chance			Good Chance				High Chance			Completely Certain

Likelihood of arresting the person and transport them to your holding facility: _____

Likelihood of arresting the person and seek to have them involuntarily committed: ____

Likelihood of an informal resolution at the scene (i.e., conflict resolution, warning): ____
Likelihood of doing nothing and leaving the scene: _____

3. While you are on patrol you receive a call for service, the dispatcher relays that the caller indicated the individual has a mental illness. According to the caller, the individual is asking for money from pedestrians and is exhibiting signs of intoxication. When you arrive on the scene you identify as a police officer and the male is responsive to your commands. Using the following scale, how likely are you to do each of the following actions?

0%		10%	20%		30%		40%	50%	60%	70%	80%	90%		100%
No Chance	Low Chance					Some Chance		Good Chance			High Chance			Completely Certain

Likelihood of arresting the person and transport them to your holding facility: _____
Likelihood of arresting the person and seek to have them involuntarily committed: ____
Likelihood of an informal resolution at the scene (i.e., conflict resolution, warning): ____
Likelihood of doing nothing and leaving the scene: _____

4. While you are on patrol you receive a call for service, the dispatcher relays that the caller indicated the individual has a mental illness. According to the caller, the individual is acting strange and threatening suicide. When you arrive on the scene you identify as a police officer and the female is responsive to your commands. Using the following scale, how likely are you to do each of the following actions?

0%		10%	20%		30%		40%	50%	60%	70%	80%	90%		100%
No Chance	Low Chance					Some Chance		Good Chance			High Chance			Completely Certain

Likelihood of arresting the person and transport them to your holding facility: _____
Likelihood of arresting the person and seek to have them involuntarily committed: ____
Likelihood of an informal resolution at the scene (i.e., conflict resolution, warning): ____
Likelihood of doing nothing and leaving the scene: _____

5. While you are on patrol you receive a call for service, the dispatcher relays that the caller indicated the individual has a mental illness.

According to the caller, the individual is asking for money from pedestrians and is exhibiting signs of intoxication. When you arrive on the scene you identify as a police officer and the female is unresponsive to you commands. Using the following scale, how likely are you to do each of the following actions?

0%		10%	20%	30%		40%	50%	60%	70%	80%	90%		100%
No Chance	Low			Some Chance			Good Chance			High			Completely
	Chance									Chance			Certain

Likelihood of arresting the person and transport them to your holding facility: _____

Likelihood of arresting the person and seek to have them involuntarily committed: _____

Likelihood of an informal resolution at the scene (i.e., conflict resolution, warning): _____

Likelihood of doing nothing and leaving the scene: _____

SECTION 2

The next set of questions are general questions about your professional and personal experience as a police officer. Check the most appropriate box. Please answer the following questions as accurately as possible.

Have you ever received any type of *mental health* or *crisis intervention training?* If yes, go to the next question, if no, skip the next question.
❑ Yes
❑ No

Did you volunteer for the *mental health* or *crisis intervention training?*
❑ Yes
❑ No

Do you know someone professionally whom you can contact for questions on mental health, or if you need help during a call for service?
❑ Yes
❑ No

Do you know someone with a serious mental illness, such as schizophrenia, bi-polar/manic, or major depressive disorder?
❑ Yes
❑ No

Have you ever had a negative experience while trying to involuntarily commit an individual?

❑ Yes

❑ No

How many years have you been a sworn police officer? If less than one year, please indicate that.

❑ _____

SECTION 3

The final section of the survey is your personal data. Please answer the questions as accurately as possible.

What is your sex?

❑ Male

❑ Female

In years, how old will you be at the conclusion of this year?

❑ _____

Which of the following racial or ethnic group do you most closely identify? *Check all that apply.*

❑ African American

❑ Asian

❑ Caucasian

❑ Hispanic/Latino

❑ Other: _____ (please indicate)

Space for comments (feel free to write next to the questions as well): _____

_____

_____

_____

_____

_____

_____

_____

_____

_____

_____

_____

_____

_____

_____

_____

_____

Time to complete: _____

Name and title: _____

_____

EXAMPLE OFFICER SURVEY

SECTION 1

Instructions: Please read each of the following scenarios. After you will be asked to answer questions about how you would respond to each situation as described in the scenario. There are no right or wrong answers.

Example: After a long week at work, Nicole and some colleagues decide to go out and have a drink at a local bar. Nicole works as a veterinary technician and has had to make tough decisions regarding the health of an animal. Using the following scale, how likely do you feel it is that Nicole would get each one of the following alcoholic drinks?

0%	10%	20%	30%	40%	50%	60%	70%	80%	90%	100%
No Chance	Low Chance		Some Chance	Good Chance				High Chance		Completely Certain

Chance of Nicole ordering hard liquor, straight: <u>25%</u>
Chance of Nicole ordering hard liquor with a mixer: <u>86%</u>
Chance of Nicole ordering a beer or hard cider: <u>71%</u>
Chance of Nicole ordering another category of drink not listed: <u>30%</u>

Begin Answering the Following Survey Questions

1. While you are on patrol you receive a call for service, the dispatcher relays that the caller indicated the individual has a mental illness. According to the caller, the individual is asking for money from pedestrians and threatening suicide. When you arrive on the scene you identify as a police officer and the male is unresponsive to your commands. Using the following scale, how likely are you to do each of the following actions?

0%	10%	20%	30%	40%	50%	60%	70%	80%	90%	100%
No Chance	Low Chance		Some Chance	Good Chance				High Chance		Completely Certain

Likelihood of arresting the person and transport them to your holding facility: _____

Likelihood of arresting the person and seek to have them involuntarily committed: ____

Likelihood of an informal resolution at the scene (i.e., conflict resolution, warning): ____

Likelihood of doing nothing and leaving the scene: _____

2. While you are on patrol you receive a call for service, the dispatcher relays that the caller indicated the individual has a mental illness. According to the caller, the individual is acting strange and arguing with objects, they appear to be hallucinating. When you arrive on the scene you identify as a police officer and the male is responsive to your commands. Using the following scale, how likely are you to do each of the following actions?

0%	10%	20%	30%	40%	50%	60%	70%	80%	90%	100%
No Chance	Low Chance		Some Chance		Good Chance			High Chance		Completely Certain

Likelihood of arresting the person and transport them to your holding facility: _____

Likelihood of arresting the person and seek to have them involuntarily committed: ____

Likelihood of an informal resolution at the scene (i.e., conflict resolution, warning): ____

Likelihood of doing nothing and leaving the scene: _____

3. While you are on patrol you receive a call for service, the dispatcher relays that the caller indicated the individual has a mental illness. According to the caller, the individual is asking for money from pedestrians and is exhibiting signs of intoxication. When you arrive on the scene you identify as a police officer and the male is responsive to your commands. Using the following scale, how likely are you to do each of the following actions?

0%	10%	20%	30%	40%	50%	60%	70%	80%	90%	100%
No Chance	Low Chance	Some Chance		Good Chance				High Chance		Completely Certain

Likelihood of arresting the person and transport them to your holding facility: _____

Likelihood of arresting the person and seek to have them involuntarily committed: ____

Likelihood of an informal resolution at the scene (i.e., conflict resolution, warning): _____
Likelihood of doing nothing and leaving the scene: _____

4. While you are on patrol you receive a call for service, the dispatcher relays that the caller indicated the individual has a mental illness. According to the caller, the individual is acting strange and threatening suicide. When you arrive on the scene you identify as a police officer and the female is responsive to your commands. Using the following scale, how likely are you to do each of the following actions?

0%		10% 20%	30%	40% 50% 60% 70%	80% 90%	100%
No Chance	Low Chance		Some Chance	Good Chance	High Chance	Completely Certain

Likelihood of arresting the person and transport them to your holding facility:
_____

Likelihood of arresting the person and seek to have them involuntarily committed: _____
Likelihood of an informal resolution at the scene (i.e., conflict resolution, warning): _____
Likelihood of doing nothing and leaving the scene: _____

5. While you are on patrol you receive a call for service, the dispatcher relays that the caller indicated the individual has a mental illness. According to the caller, the individual is asking for money from pedestrians and is exhibiting signs of intoxication. When you arrive on the scene you identify as a police officer and the female is unresponsive to your commands. Using the following scale, how likely are you to do each of the following actions?

0%		10% 20%	30%	40% 50% 60% 70%	80% 90%	100%
No Chance	Low Chance		Some Chance	Good Chance	High Chance	Completely Certain

Likelihood of arresting the person and transport them to your holding facility:
_____

Likelihood of arresting the person and seek to have them involuntarily committed: _____
Likelihood of an informal resolution at the scene (i.e., conflict resolution, warning): _____
Likelihood of doing nothing and leaving the scene: _____

SECTION 2

The next set of questions are general questions about your professional and personal experience as a police officer. Check the most appropriate box. Please answer the following questions as accurately as possible.

Have you ever received any type of *mental health* or *crisis intervention training?* If yes, go to the next question, if no, skip the next question.
❑ Yes
❑ No
Did you volunteer for the *mental health* or *crisis intervention training?*
❑ Yes
❑ No
Do you know someone professionally whom you can contact for questions on mental health, or if you need help during a call for service?
❑ Yes
❑ No
Do you know someone with a serious mental illness, such as schizophrenia, bi-polar/manic, or major depressive disorder?
❑ Yes
❑ No
Have you ever had a negative experience while trying to involuntarily commit an individual?
❑ Yes
❑ No
❑ Not Applicable
Think of the place you patrol most frequently, how would you categorize that area?
❑ Urban
❑ Suburban
❑ Rural
How would you classify the size of your department?
❑ Small (oversees a population of 9,999 citizens or less)
❑ Medium (oversees a population of 10,000 to 99,999 citizens)
❑ Large (oversees a population of 100,000 or more)
How many years have you been a sworn police officer? If less than one year, please indicate that.
❑ _____

SECTION 3

The final section of the survey is your personal data. Please answer the questions as accurately as possible.

What is your sex?
❏ Male
❏ Female
In years, how old will you be at the conclusion of this year?
❏ _____
Which of the following racial or ethnic group do you most closely identify?
Check all that apply.
❏ African American
❏ Caucasian
❏ Hispanic/Latino
❏ Asian
❏ Other: _____ (please indicate)
Please write in the County and State in which your department jurisdiction falls.
❏   _____

_____

EXAMPLE CADET SURVEY

SECTION 1

Instructions: Please read each of the following scenarios. After you will be asked to answer questions about how you would respond to each situation as described in the scenario. There are no right or wrong answers.
    Example: After a long week at work, Nicole and some colleagues decide to go out and have a drink at a local bar. Nicole works as a veterinary technician and has had to make tough decisions regarding the health of an animal. Using the following scale, how likely do you feel it is that Nicole would get each one of the following alcoholic drinks?

0%	10%	20%	30%	40%	50%	60%	70%	80%	90%	100%
No Chance	Low Chance		Some Chance		Good Chance			High Chance		Completely Certain

Chance of Nicole ordering hard liquor, straight: <u>25%</u>
Chance of Nicole ordering hard liquor with a mixer: <u>86%</u>
Chance of Nicole ordering a beer or hard cider: <u>71%</u>
Chance of Nicole ordering another category of drink not listed: <u>30%</u>

Begin Answering the Following Survey Questions

1. While you are on patrol you receive a call for service, the dispatcher relays that the caller indicated the individual has a mental illness. According to the caller, the individual is asking for money from pedestrians and threatening suicide. When you arrive on the scene you identify as a police officer and the male is unresponsive to your commands. Using the following scale, how likely are you to do each of the following actions?

0%		10% 20%	30%	40% 50% 60% 70%	80% 90%	100%
No Chance	Low		Some Chance	Good Chance	High	Completely
	Chance				Chance	Certain

Likelihood of arresting the person and transport them to your holding facility: _____

Likelihood of arresting the person and seek to have them involuntarily committed: ____

Likelihood of an informal resolution at the scene (i.e., conflict resolution, warning): ____

Likelihood of doing nothing and leaving the scene: _____

2. While you are on patrol you receive a call for service, the dispatcher relays that the caller indicated the individual has a mental illness. According to the caller, the individual is acting strange and arguing with objects, they appear to be hallucinating. When you arrive on the scene you identify as a police officer and the male is responsive to your commands. Using the following scale, how likely are you to do each of the following actions?

0%		10% 20%	30%	40% 50% 60% 70%	80% 90%	100%
No Chance	Low		Some Chance	Good Chance	High	Completely
	Chance				Chance	Certain

Likelihood of arresting the person and transport them to your holding facility: _____

Likelihood of arresting the person and seek to have them involuntarily committed: ____

Likelihood of an informal resolution at the scene (i.e., conflict resolution, warning): ____

Likelihood of doing nothing and leaving the scene: _____

3. While you are on patrol you receive a call for service, the dispatcher relays that the caller indicated the individual has a mental illness. According to the caller, the individual is asking for money from pedestrians and is exhibiting signs of intoxication. When you arrive on the scene you identify

as a police officer and the male is responsive to your commands. Using the following scale, how likely are you to do each of the following actions?

0%		10%	20%	30%		40%	50%	60%	70%	80%	90%		100%
No Chance	Low Chance			Some Chance			Good Chance			High Chance			Completely Certain

Likelihood of arresting the person and transport them to your holding facility: _____

Likelihood of arresting the person and seek to have them involuntarily committed: _____

Likelihood of an informal resolution at the scene (i.e., conflict resolution, warning): _____

Likelihood of doing nothing and leaving the scene: _____

4. While you are on patrol you receive a call for service, the dispatcher relays that the caller indicated the individual has a mental illness. According to the caller, the individual is acting strange and threatening suicide. When you arrive on the scene you identify as a police officer and the female is responsive to your commands. Using the following scale, how likely are you to do each of the following actions?

0%		10%	20%	30%		40%	50%	60%	70%	80%	90%		100%
No Chance	Low Chance			Some Chance			Good Chance			High Chance			Completely Certain

Likelihood of arresting the person and transport them to your holding facility: _____

Likelihood of arresting the person and seek to have them involuntarily committed: _____

Likelihood of an informal resolution at the scene (i.e., conflict resolution, warning): _____

Likelihood of doing nothing and leaving the scene: _____

5. While you are on patrol you receive a call for service, the dispatcher relays that the caller indicated the individual has a mental illness. According to the caller, the individual is asking for money from pedestrians and is exhibiting signs of intoxication. When you arrive on the scene you identify as a police officer and the female is unresponsive to your commands. Using the following scale, how likely are you to do each of the following actions?

0%		10%	20%	30%	40%	50%	60%	70%	80%	90%	100%
No Chance	Low Chance		Some Chance		Good Chance				High Chance		Completely Certain

Likelihood of arresting the person and transport them to your holding facility: _____

Likelihood of arresting the person and seek to have them involuntarily committed: ____

Likelihood of an informal resolution at the scene (i.e., conflict resolution, warning): ____

Likelihood of doing nothing and leaving the scene: _____

SECTION 2

The next set of questions are general questions about your professional and personal experience as a police officer. Check the most appropriate box. Please answer the following questions as accurately as possible.

Have you ever received any type of *mental health* or *crisis intervention training*? If yes, go to the next question, if no, skip the next question.
❑ Yes
❑ No
Did you volunteer for the *mental health* or *crisis intervention training*?
❑ Yes
❑ No
During your courses at the Criminal Justice Training Center, have you discussed or been trained on dealing with individuals who appear to have a mental illness?
❑ Yes
❑ No
Do you know someone professionally whom you can contact for questions on mental health, or if you need help during a call for service?
❑ Yes
❑ No
Do you know someone with a serious mental illness, such as schizophrenia, bi-polar/manic, or major depressive disorder?
❑ Yes
❑ No
How many weeks have you been attending courses at the Criminal Justice Training Center?
❑ _____

SECTION 3

The final section of the survey is your personal data. Please answer the questions as accurately as possible.

What is your sex?
❑ Male
❑ Female
In years, how old will you be at the conclusion of this year?
❑ _____
Which of the following racial or ethnic group do you most closely identify?
   Check all that apply.
❑ African American
❑ Asian
❑ Caucasian
❑ Hispanic/Latino
❑ Other: _____ (please indicate)

No Chance	Low Chance	Some Chance	Good Chance	High Chance	Completely Certain
0	20	40	60	80	100

Arrest with transportation to holding facility

Detainment with transportation to hospital for involuntary commitment assessment

Informal resolution at the scene (ie: warning)

No action or leaving the scene

<< >>

Appendix C

Vignette Universe

1. While you are on patrol you receive a call for service, the dispatcher relays that the caller indicated the individual has a mental illness. According to the caller, there is an individual who is asking for money from pedestrians and threatening suicide. When you arrive on the scene you identify as a police officer and the male is unresponsive to your commands. Using the following scale, how likely are you to do each of the following actions?

2. While you are on patrol you receive a call for service, the dispatcher relays that the caller indicated the individual has a mental illness. According to the caller, there is an individual who is acting strange and threatening suicide. When you arrive on the scene you identify as a police officer and the male is unresponsive to your commands. Using the following scale, how likely are you to do each of the following actions?

3. While you are on patrol you receive a call for service, the dispatcher relays that the caller indicated the individual has a mental illness. According to the caller, there is an individual who is asking for money from pedestrians and threatening suicide. When you arrive on the scene you identify as a police officer and the male is responsive to your commands. Using the following scale, how likely are you to do each of the following actions?

4. While you are on patrol you receive a call for service, the dispatcher relays that the caller indicated the individual has a mental illness. According to the caller, there is an individual who is acting strange and threatening suicide. When you arrive on the scene you identify as a police officer and the male is responsive to your commands. Using the following scale, how likely are you to do each of the following actions?

5. While you are on patrol you receive a call for service, the dispatcher relays that the caller indicated the individual has a mental illness. According to the caller, there is an individual who is asking for money from pedestrians and arguing with objects and appears to be hallucinating. When you arrive on the scene you identify as a police officer and the male is unresponsive to your commands. Using the following scale, how likely are you to do each of the following actions?

6. While you are on patrol you receive a call for service, the dispatcher relays that the caller indicated the individual has a mental illness. According to the caller, there is an individual who is acting strange and arguing with objects and appears to be hallucinating. When you arrive on the scene you identify as a police officer and the male is unresponsive to your commands. Using the following scale, how likely are you to do each of the following actions?

7. While you are on patrol you receive a call for service, the dispatcher relays that the caller indicated the individual has a mental illness. According to the caller, there is an individual who is asking for money from pedestrians and arguing with objects and appears to be hallucinating. When you arrive on the scene you identify as a police officer and the male is responsive to your commands. Using the following scale, how likely are you to do each of the following actions?

8. While you are on patrol you receive a call for service, the dispatcher relays that the caller indicated the individual has a mental illness. According to the caller, there is an individual who is acting strange and arguing with objects and appears to be hallucinating. When you arrive on the scene you identify as a police officer and the male is responsive to your commands. Using the following scale, how likely are you to do each of the following actions?

9. While you are on patrol you receive a call for service, the dispatcher relays that the caller indicated the individual has a mental illness. According to the caller, there is an individual who is asking for money from pedestrians and person is exhibiting signs of intoxication. When you arrive on the scene you identify as a police officer and the male is unresponsive to your commands. Using the following scale, how likely are you to do each of the following actions?

10. While you are on patrol you receive a call for service, the dispatcher relays that the caller indicated the individual has a mental illness. According to the caller, there is an individual who is acting strange and the person is exhibiting signs of intoxication. When you arrive on the scene you identify as a police officer and the male is unresponsive to your commands. Using the following scale, how likely are you to do each of the following actions?

11. While you are on patrol you receive a call for service, the dispatcher relays that the caller indicated the individual has a mental illness. According to the caller, there is an individual who is asking for money from pedestrians and the person is exhibiting signs of intoxication. When you arrive on the scene you identify as a police officer and the male is responsive to your commands. Using the following scale, how likely are you to do each of the following actions?

12. While you are on patrol you receive a call for service, the dispatcher relays that the caller indicated the individual has a mental illness. According to the caller, there is an individual who is acting strange and the person is exhibiting signs of intoxication. When you arrive on the scene you identify as a police officer and the male is responsive to your commands. Using the following scale, how likely are you to do each of the following actions?

13. While you are on patrol you receive a call for service, the dispatcher relays that the caller indicated the individual has a mental illness. According to the caller, there is an individual who is asking for money from pedestrians and threatening suicide. When you arrive on the scene you identify as a police officer and the female is unresponsive to your commands. Using the following scale, how likely are you to do each of the following actions?

14. While you are on patrol you receive a call for service, the dispatcher relays that the caller indicated the individual has a mental illness. According to the caller, there is an individual who is acting strange and threatening suicide. When you arrive on the scene you identify as a police officer and the female is unresponsive to your commands. Using the following scale, how likely are you to do each of the following actions?

15. While you are on patrol you receive a call for service, the dispatcher relays that the caller indicated the individual has a mental illness. According to the caller, there is an individual who is asking for money from pedestrians and threatening suicide. When you arrive on the scene you identify as a police officer and the female is responsive to your commands. Using the following scale, how likely are you to do each of the following actions?

16. While you are on patrol you receive a call for service, the dispatcher relays that the caller indicated the individual has a mental illness. According to the caller, there is an individual who is acting strange and threatening suicide. When you arrive on the scene you identify as a police officer and the female is responsive to your commands. Using the following scale, how likely are you to do each of the following actions?

17. While you are on patrol you receive a call for service, the dispatcher relays that the caller indicated the individual has a mental illness.

According to the caller, there is an individual who is asking for money from pedestrians and arguing with objects and appears to be hallucinating. When you arrive on the scene you identify as a police officer and the female is unresponsive to your commands. Using the following scale, how likely are you to do each of the following actions?

18. While you are on patrol you receive a call for service, the dispatcher relays that the caller indicated the individual has a mental illness. According to the caller, there is an individual who is acting strange and arguing with objects and appears to be hallucinating. When you arrive on the scene you identify as a police officer and the female is unresponsive to your commands. Using the following scale, how likely are you to do each of the following actions?

19. While you are on patrol you receive a call for service, the dispatcher relays that the caller indicated the individual has a mental illness. According to the caller, there is an individual who is asking for money from pedestrians and arguing with objects and appears to be hallucinating. When you arrive on the scene you identify as a police officer and the female is responsive to your commands. Using the following scale, how likely are you to do each of the following actions?

20. While you are on patrol you receive a call for service, the dispatcher relays that the caller indicated the individual has a mental illness. According to the caller, there is an individual who is acting strange and arguing with objects and appears to be hallucinating. When you arrive on the scene you identify as a police officer and the female is responsive to your commands. Using the following scale, how likely are you to do each of the following actions?

21. While you are on patrol you receive a call for service, the dispatcher relays that the caller indicated the individual has a mental illness. According to the caller, there is an individual who is asking for money from pedestrians and person is exhibiting signs of intoxication. When you arrive on the scene you identify as a police officer and the female is unresponsive to your commands. Using the following scale, how likely are you to do each of the following actions?

22. While you are on patrol you receive a call for service, the dispatcher relays that the caller indicated the individual has a mental illness. According to the caller, there is an individual who is acting strange and the person is exhibiting signs of intoxication. When you arrive on the scene you identify as a police officer and the female is unresponsive to your commands. Using the following scale, how likely are you to do each of the following actions?

23. While you are on patrol you receive a call for service, the dispatcher relays that the caller indicated the individual has a mental illness.

According to the caller, there is an individual who is asking for money from pedestrians and the person is exhibiting signs of intoxication. When you arrive on the scene you identify as a police officer and the female is responsive to your commands. Using the following scale, how likely are you to do each of the following actions?

24. While you are on patrol you receive a call for service, the dispatcher relays that the caller indicated the individual has a mental illness. According to the caller, there is an individual who is acting strange and the person is exhibiting signs of intoxication. When you arrive on the scene you identify as a police officer and the female is responsive to your commands. Using the following scale, how likely are you to do each of the following actions?

References

Abramson, M. F. (1972). The criminalization of mentally disordered behavior: Possible side-effect of a new mental health law. *Psychiatric Services*, *23*(4), 101–105.

Accordino, M. P., Porter, D. F., & Morse, T. (2001). Deinstitutionalization of persons with severe mental illness: Context and consequences. *Journal of Rehabilitation*, *67*(2), 16–21.

Adams, K., & Ferrandino, J. (2008). Managing mentally ill inmates in prisons. *Criminal Justice and Behavior*, *35*, 913–927.

Akins, S., Burkhardt, B., Lanfear, C., Amorim, M., & Stevens, K. (2014). Law enforcement response to people with mental illnesses in Benton County. Retrieved from http://www.co.benton.or.us/da/wcjc/documents.php Google Scholar

Almquist, L., & Dodd, E. (2009). *Mental health courts: A guide to research-informed policy and practice*. New York, NY: Justice Center, The Council of State Governments, Bureau of Justice Assistance.

Amagoh, F. (2008). Perspectives on organizational change: Systems and complexity theories. *The Innovation Journal: The Public Sector Innovation Journal*, *13*(3), 1–14.

American Psychiatric Association. (2000). *Diagnostic and statistical manual of mental disorders* (4th ed., text rev.). Washington, D.C.: Author.

Antonio, M. E., Young, J. L., & Wingeard, L. M. (2009). When actions and attitude count most: Assessing perceived level of responsibility and support for inmate treatment and rehabilitation programs among correctional employees. *Prison Journal*, *89*, 363–382. doi:10.1177/0032885509349554

Atzmuller, C., & Steiner, P. M. (2010). Experimental vignette studies in survey research. *Methodology*, *6*(3), 128–138.

Auspurg, K., & Hinz, T. (2016). *Factorial survey experiments*. Los Angeles, CA: Sage.

Bachman, R., & Schutt, R. K. (2010). *The practice of research in criminology and criminal justice*. Thousand Oaks, CA: SAGE Inc.

Banks, D., Hendrix, J., Hickman, M., & Kyckelhahn, T. (2016). *National sources of law enforcement employment data* (Report No. NCJ249681). Washington, D.C.: U.S. Department of Justice, Bureau of Justice Statistics.

Benton, D., & Masciadrelli, B. P. (2013). Legitimacy of correction as a mental health care provider: Perspectives from U.S. and European systems. *Journal of the Institute of Justice and International Studies, 13*, 1–15.

Bergner, R. M., & Bunford, N. (2017). Mental disorder is a disability concept, not a behavioral one. *Philosophy, Psychiatry, & Psychology, 24*(1), 25–40.

Bittner, E. (1967). Police discretion in emergency apprehension of mentally ill persons. *Social Problems, 14*(3), 278–292.

Blitz, C. L., Wolff, N., & Shi, J. (2008). Physical victimization in prison: The role of mental illness. *International Journal of Law and Psychiatry, 31*(5), 385–393.

Bolton, D. (2008). *What is mental disorder? An essay in philosophy, science, and values.* New York, NY: Oxford University Press.

Borum, R., Deane, M. W., Steadman, H. J., & Morrissey, J. (1998). Police perspectives on responding to mentally ill people in crisis: Perceptions of program effectiveness. *Mental Health Law & Policy Faculty Publications, 16*, 393–405.

Bower, D. L., & Pettit, G. W. (2001). Albuquerque Police Department's crisis intervention team: A report card. *FBI Law Enforcement Bulletin, 70*(2), 1–6.

Bronson, J., & Berzofsky, M. (2018). *Indicator of mental health problems reported by prisoners and jail inmates, 2011–12* (Report No. NCJ 250612). Washington, D.C.: U.S. Department of Justice, Bureau of Justice Statistics.

Burt, R. S. (1992). *Structural holes: The social structure of competition.* Cambridge, MA: Harvard University Press.

Cappellazzo, T. M. (2016). Police interactions with mentally ill individuals. *Sociological Imagination: Western's Undergraduate Sociological Student Journal, 5*(1), Art. 2, 1–12.

Carey, K. B., & Correia, C. J. (1998). Severe mental illness and addictions: Assessment considerations. *Addictive Behaviors, 23*(6), 735–748.

Castellano, U., & Anderson, L. (2013). Mental health courts in America. *American Behavioral Scientist, 57*(2), 163–173. doi:10.1177/0002764212465616

Chaimowitz, G. (2011). The criminalization of people with mental illness. *The Canadian Journal of Psychiatry, 57*(2), 1–6.

Cohen, L. E., & Felson, M. (1979). Social change and crime rate trends: A routine activity approach. *American Sociological Review, 44*(4), 588–608.

Coleman, T. G., & Cotton, D. H. (2010). Reducing risk and improving outcomes of police interactions with people with mental illness. *Journal of Police Crisis Negotiations, 10*, 39–57.

Compton, M. T., Broussard, B., Reed, T. A., Crisafio, A., & Watson, A. C. (2015). Surveys of police chiefs and sheriffs and of police officers about CIT programs. *Psychiatry Services, 66*(7), 760–763.

Compton, W. M., Thomas, Y. F., Stinson, F. S., & Grant, B. F. (2007). Prevalence, correlates, disability, and comorbidity of DSM-IV drug abuse and dependence in the United States. *Archives of General Psychiatry, 64*(5), 566–576.

Constantine, R., Andel, R., Petrilea, J., Becker, M., Robst, J., Teague, G., & Howe, A. (2010). Characteristics and experiences of adults with a serious mental illness who were involved in the criminal justice system. *Psychiatric Service, 64*(5), 451–457.

Cooper, J. A. (2012). *Examining the diffusion of police arrests across urban space: Territoriality, the police role, and isomorphism* (Doctoral dissertation) (UMI No. 3517979). Ann Arbor, MI: ProQuest.

Cooper, J. A. (2015). *Twentieth-century influences on twenty-first-century policing: Continued lessons of police reform.* Lanham, MD: Lexington Books.

Cooper, J. A., & Garson, G. D. (2016). *Power analysis.* Asheboro, NC: Statistical Associates Publishers.

Cooper, J. A., White, M. D., Ward, K. C., Raganella, A. J., & Saunders, J. (2014). Exploring the nexus of officer race/ethnicity, sex, and job satisfaction: The case of the NYPD. *Criminology, Criminal Justice Law & Society, 15*(2), 43–59.

Cooper, V. G., McLearen, A. M., & Zapf, P. A. (2004). Dispositional decisions with the mentally ill: Police perceptions and characteristics. *Police Quarterly, 7*(3), 295–310.

Cordner, G. (2006). *People with mental illness* (Report No. 40). Washington, D.C.: U.S. Department of Justice, Office of Community Oriented Policing Services.

Cornelius, L. J., Simpson, G. M., Ting, L., Wiggins, E., & Lipford, S. (2003). Reach out and I'll be there: Mental health crisis intervention and mobile outreach services to urban African Americans. *Health & Social Work, 28*(1), 74–78.

Davidson, M. L. (2016). A criminal justice system-wide response to mental illness: Evaluating the effectiveness of the Memphis Crisis Intervention Team training curriculum among law enforcement and correctional officers. *Criminal Justice Policy Review, 27*(1), 46–75.

Davis, E., Whyde, A., & Langton, L. (2018). *Contacts between police and the public, 2015* (Report No. NCJ 251145). Washington, D.C.: U.S. Department of Justice, Bureau of Justice Statistics.

Davis, L., Fulginiti, A., Kriegal, L., & Brekke, J. (2012). Deinstitutionalization? Where have all people gone? *Current Psychiatry Report, 14,* 259–269. doi:10.1007/s11920-012-0271-1

Dilulio, J. J. (1993). Measuring performance when there is no bottom line. In J. J. DiIulio (Ed.), *Performance measures for the criminal justice system* (pp. 147–160). Washington, D.C.: U.S. Government Printing Office.

Dvoskin, J. A., & Spiers, E. M. (2004). On the role of correctional officers in prison mental health. *Psychiatric Quarterly, 75*(1), 41–59.

Engel, R. S., & Silver, R. (2001). Policing mentally disordered suspects: A reexamination of the criminalization hypothesis. *Criminology, 39*(2), 225–252.

Farrokhi, F., & Mahmoudi-Hamidabad, A. (2012). Rethinking convenience sampling: Defining quality criteria. *Theory and Practice in Language Studies, 2*(4), 784–792.

Ferber, R. (1977). Research by convenience. *Journal of Consumer Research, 4*(1), 57–58.

Fields, J. D. (1976). O'Connor v. Donaldson. *Hofstra Law Review, 4*(2), 1–20.

Fisher, W. H., Silver, E., & Wolff, N. (2006). Beyond criminalization: Toward a criminologically informed framework for mental health policy and services research. *Administration and Policy in Mental Health and Mental Health Services Research, 33*, 544–557. doi:10.1007/s10488-006-0072-0

Geiman, D. (2007). Managing inmates with mental health disorders. *Corrections Today, 69*, 22–23.

Goldman, H. H., & Grob, G. N. (2006). Defining 'mental illness' in mental health policy. *Health Affairs, 25*(3), 737–749. doi:10.1377/hlthaff.25.3.737

Goldstein, H. (1979). Improving policing: A problem-oriented approach. *Crime & Delinquency, 25*(2), 236–258.

Gonzales, V. M., Bradizza, C. M., Vincent, P. C., Stasiewicz, P. R., & Paas, N. D. (2007). Do individuals with a severe mental illness experience greater alcohol and drug-related problems? A test of the supersensitivity hypothesis. *Addictive Behaviors, 32*, 477–490.

Granello, D. H., & Granello, P. F. (2000). Defining mental illness: The relationship between college students' beliefs about the definition of mental illness and tolerance. *Journal of College Counseling, 3*(2), 100–112.

Granovetter, M. S. (1973). The strength of weak ties. *American Journal of Sociology, 78*(6), 1360–1380.

Gronfein, W. (1985). Incentives and intentions in mental health policy: A comparison of the Medicaid and community mental health programs. *Journal of Health and Social Behavior, 26*(3), 192–206.

Gur, O. M. (2010). Persons with mental health illness in the criminal justice system: Police interventions to prevent violence and criminalization. *Journal of Police Crisis Negotiations, 10*, 220–240. doi:10.1080/15332581003799752

Harcourt, B. E. (2011). Reducing mass incarceration: Lessons from the deinstitutionalization of mental hospitals in the 1960s. *University of Chicago Public Law and Legal Theory Working Paper, 335*, 1–32.

Harmening, W. M. (2014). *Crisis intervention: The criminal justice response to chaos, mayhem, and disorder.* Upper Saddle River, NJ: Pearson.

Helfgott, J. B., Hickman, M. J., & Labossiere, A. P. (2016). A descriptive evaluation of the Seattle Police Department's crisis response team officer/mental health professional partnership pilot program. *International Journal of Law and Psychiatry, 44*, 109–122.

Hiday, V. A., & Ray, B. (2010). Arrests two years after exiting a well-established mental health court. *Psychiatric Services, 61*(5), 463–468.

Humphreys, K., & Rappaport, J. (1993). From the community mental health movement to the war on drugs. *American Psychologist, 48*(8), 892–901.

Jachimowski, K. G. (2018a). *Police response to mental health calls for service.* Unpublished doctoral dissertation, Indiana University of Pennsylvania, Indiana, Pennsylvania.

Jachimowski, K. G. (2018b). The relationship between mentally disordered inmates, victimization, and violence. *Journal Offender Rehabilitation, 57*(1), 47–65. doi:10.1080/10509674.2017.1416438

Jachimowski, K. G., & Smathers, C. J. (2019). Mental health and CIT in a prison setting. In J. A. Cooper & K. G. Jachimowski (Eds.), *A closer look at criminal justice* (pp. 199–227). New York, NY: Nova Science Publishers Inc.

James, D. L., & Glaze, L. E. (2006). *Mental health problems of prison and jail inmates* (Report No. NCJ 213600). Washington, D.C.: U.S. Department of Justice, Bureau of Justice Statistics.

Jennings, W. G., & Hudak, E. J. (2005). Police responses to persons with mental illness. In R. G. Dunham & G. P. Alpert (Eds.), *Critical issues in policing: Contemporary readings* (5th ed., pp. 115–128). Long Grove, IL: Waveland.

Johnson, R. R. (2011). Suspect mental disorder and police use of force. *Criminal Justice & Behavior, 38*(2), 127–145.

Jones, M. M. (2015). Creating a science of homelessness during the Reagan era. *The Milbank Quarterly, 93*(1), 139–178.

Keown, P., Tacchi, M. J., Niemiec, S., & Hughes, J. (2007). Changes to mental healthcare for working age adults: Impact of a crisis team and an assertive outreach team. *Psychiatric Bulletin, 31*, 288–292. doi:10.1192/pb.bp.106.012054

Kerle, K. (2016). The mentally ill and crisis intervention teams: Reflections on jails and the U.S. mental health challenge. *The Prison Journal, 96*(1), 153–161.

Kesic, D., Thomas, S. D., & Ogloff, J. R. (2010). Mental illness among police fatalities in Victoria 1982–2007: Case linkage study. *Australian and New Zealand Journal of Psychiatry, 44*(5), 463–468.

Kim, D. (2014). Psychiatric deinstitutionalization and prison population growth: A critical literature review and its implications. *Criminal Justice Policy Review, 27*(1), 3–21. doi:10.1177/0887403414547043

Kisely, S., Campbell, L. A., Peddle, S., Hare, S., Pyche, M., Spicer, D., & Moore, B. (2010). A controlled before-and-after evaluation of a mobile crisis partnership between mental health and police services in Nova Scotia. *La Revue canadienne de psychiatrie, 55*(10), 662–668.

Klinger, D. A. (1996). Quantifying law in police-citizen encounters. *Journal of Quantitative Criminology, 12*, 391–415.

Klofas, J., Hipple, N. K., & McGarrell, E. (2010). *The new criminal justice: American communities and the changing world of crime control.* New York, NY: Routledge.

Kois, L. E., Hill, K., Gonzales, L., Hunter, S., & Chauhan, P. (2020). Correctional officer mental health training: Analysis of 52 U.S. Jurisdictions. *Criminal Justice Policy Review, 31*(4), 55–572.

Lamb, H. R. (1984). Deinstitutionalization and the homeless mentally ill. *Hospital and Community Psychiatry, 35*(9), 899–907.

Lee, S. J., Thomas, P., Doulis, C., Bowles, D., Henderson, K., Keppich-Arnold, S., Perez, E., & Stafrace, S. (2015). Outcomes achieved by and police and clinician perspectives on a joint police officer and mental health clinician mobile response unit. *International Journal of Mental Health Nursing, 24*, 538–546. doi:10.1111/inm.12153

Livingston, J. D., Desmarais, S. L., Greaves, C., Parent, R., Verdun-Jones, S., & Brink, J. (2014b). What influences perceptions of procedural justice among people with mental illness regarding their interactions with the police? *Community Mental Health, 50,* 281–287.

Livingston, J. D., Desmarais, S. L., Verdun-Jones, S., Parent, R., Michalak, E., & Brink, J. (2014a). Perceptions and experience of people with mental illness regarding their interactions with police. *International Journal of Law & Psychiatry, 37,* 334–340.

Lord, V. B., & Bjerregaard, B. (2014). Helping persons with mental illness: Partnerships between police and mobile crisis units. *Victims and Offenders, 9,* 455–474. doi:10.1080/15564886.2013.878263

Luke, D. A. (2011). *Multilevel modeling.* Thousand Oaks, CA: SAGE Inc.

Lurigio, A. J. (2013). Forty years after Abramson: Beliefs about the criminalization of people with serious mental illnesses. *International Journal of Offender Therapy and Comparative Criminology, 57*(7), 763–765. doi:10.1177/0306624x13490142

Lynum, K. S., & Hill, A. M. (2015). Psychiatric services: A platform for MTM. *Journal of Pharmacy Practice, 28*(1), 13–20. doi:10.1177/0897190014562352

Markowitz, F. E., & Watson, A. C. (2015). Police response to domestic violence: Situations involving veterans exhibiting signs of mental illness. *Criminology, 53*(2), 231–252.

Matthews, L. J. (2016). A broken outline—Being an observer in my own life: Notes from a service user. In J. Winstone (Ed.), *Mental health, crime, and criminal justice: Responses and reforms* (pp. 21–27). Hampshire: Palgrave Macmillan.

McLean, N., & Marshall, L. A. (2010). A front line police perspective of mental health issues and services. *Criminal Behaviour and Mental Health, 20,* 62–71. doi:10.1002/cbm.756

McNally, R. J. (2012). *What is mental illness?* Cambridge, MA: Harvard University Press.

McNeil, D. E., & Binder, R. L. (2007). Effectiveness of a mental health court in reducing criminal recidivism and violence. *The American Journal of Psychiatry, 164*(9), 1395–1403.

Mechanic, D. (2007). Barriers to help-seeking, detection, and adequate treatment for anxiety and mood disorders: Implications for health care policy. *The Journal of Clinical Psychiatry, 68*(Suppl. 2), 20–26.

Mechanic, D., & Rochefort, D. A. (1990). Deinstitutionalization: An appraisal of reform. *The Annual Review of Sociology, 16,* 301–327.

Miller, J., Davis, R. C., Henderson, N. J., Markovic, J., & Ortiz, C. W. (2004). *Public opinions of the police: The influence of friends, family, and news media.* New York, NY: Vera Institute of Justice.

Montross, C. (2016). Hard time or hospital treatment? Mental illness and the criminal justice system. *The New England Journal of Medicine, 375*(15), 1407–1409.

Moore, L. D., & Elkavich, A. (2008). Who's using and who's doing time: Incarceration, the war on drugs, and public health. *American Journal of Public Health, 98*(5), 782–786.

Morabito, M. S., Kerr, A. N., Watson, A., Draine, J., Ottati, V., & Angell, B. (2010). Crisis intervention teams and people with mental illness. *Crime & Delinquency, 58*(1), 57–77.

Morabito, M. S., & Socia, K. M. (2015). Is dangerousness a myth? Injuries and police encounters with people with mental illness. *Criminology & Public Policy, 14*(2), 1–24.

Morgan, G. (1998). *Images of organization.* Thousand Oaks, CA: Sage Publications.

Muijs, D. (2011). *Doing quantitative research in education with SPSS* (2nd ed.). Thousand Oaks, CA: SAGE Inc.

Muir, W. K. (1977). *Police: Streetcorner politicians.* Chicago: University of Chicago Press.

Murphy, K. (2012). Crisis intervention teams and mobile crisis management. *North Carolina Medical Journal, 73*(3), 200.

O'Connor v. Donaldson. (1975). 422 US 563, 95 S. *Ct, 2486,* 45.

Packer, H. L. (1964). Two models of the criminal process. *University of Pennsylvania Law Review, 13*(1), 1–68.

Pare, P., & Logan, M. W. (2011). Risk of minor and serious violent victimization in prison: The impact of inmates mental disorders, physical disabilities, and physical size. *Society and Mental Health, 1,* 106–123.

Parker, G. F. (2009). Impact of a mental health training course for correctional officers on a special housing unit. *Psychiatric Services, 60*(5), 640–645.

Peplau, H. E. (1992). Interpersonal relations: A theoretical framework for application in nursing practice. *Nursing Science Quarterly, 5*(1), 13–18.

Peplau, H. E. (1997). Peplau's theory of interpersonal relations. *Nursing Science Quarterly, 10*(4), 162–167.

Perez, A., Leifman, S., & Estrada, A. (2003). Reversing the criminalization of mental illness. *Crime & Delinquency, 49*(1), 62–78. doi:10.1177/0011128702239236

Pfeiffer, M. B. (2007). Mentally ill inmates face a cruel system. *Corrections Forum, 16,* 60–62.

Prigmore, C. S., & Davis, P. R. (1973). Wyatt v. Stickney: Rights of the committed. *Social Work, 18*(4), 10–18.

Prin, S. J. (2014). Prevalence of mental illness in U.S. state prisons: A systematic review. *Psychiatric Service, 65*(7), 862–872.

Raganella, A. J., & White, M. D. (2004). Race, gender, and motivation for becoming a police officer: Implications for building a representative police department. *Journal of Criminal Justice, 32,* 501–513.

Ray, B. (2014). Long-term recidivism of mental health court defendants. *International Journal of Law and Psychiatry, 37,* 448–454. doi:10.1016/j.ijlp.2014.02.017

Reiger, D. A., Farmer, M. E., Rae, D. S., Locke, B. Z., Keith, S. J., Judd, L. L., & Goodwin, F. K. (1990). Comorbidity of mental disorders with alcohol and other drug abuse: Results from the epidemiologic catchment area (ECA) study. *JAMA, 264*(19), 2511–2518.

Reuland, M., Draper, L., & Norton, B. (2013). Developing a statewide approach to specialized policing response (SPR) programme implementation. In D. Chappel (Ed.), *Policing and the mentally ill: International perspectives* (pp. 3–18). Boca Raton, FL: CRC Press.

Reuland, M., Schwarzfeld, M., & Draper, L. (2009). *Law enforcement responses to people with mental illnesses: A guide to research-informed policy and practice.* New York, NY: Council of State Governments Justice Center.

Richman, A., Wilson, K., Scally, L., Edwards, P., & Wood, J. (2003). An outreach support team for older people with mental illness—Crisis intervention. *Psychiatric Bulletin, 27,* 348–351.

Ringhoff, D., Rapp, L., & Robst, J. (2012). The criminalization hypothesis: Practice and policy implications for persons with serious mental illness in the criminal justice system. *Best Practices in Mental Health, 8*(2), 1–19.

Ritter, C., Teller, J. L., Marcussen, K., Munetz, M. R., & Teasdale, B. (2011). Crisis intervention team officer dispatch, assessment, and disposition: Interactions with individuals with severe mental illness. *International Journal of Law and Psychiatry, 34*(1), 30–38.

Robinson, J., Sareen, J., Cox, B. J., & Bolton, J. (2009). Self-medication of anxiety disorders with alcohol and drugs: Results from a nationally representative sample. *Journal of Anxiety Disorders, 23,* 38–45. doi:10.1016/j.janxdis.2008.03.013

Rochefort, D. A. (1984). Origins of the "third psychiatric revolution": The community mental health centers act of 1963. *Journal of Health Politics, Policy and Law, 9*(1), 1–29.

Rosenbaum, N. (2010). Street-level psychiatry—A psychiatrist's role with the Albuquerque police department's crisis outreach and support team. *Journal of Police Crisis Negotiations, 10,* 175–181.

Ruiz, J., & Miller, C. (2004). An exploratory study of Pennsylvania police officers' perceptions of dangerousness and their ability to manage persons with mental illness. *Police Quarterly, 7*(3), 359–371. doi:10.1177/1098611103258957

Scheff, T. J. (1966). Users and non-users of a student psychiatric clinic. *Journal of Health and Human Behavior, 7*(2), 114–121.

Schulenberg, J. L. (2015). Police decision-making in the gray zone: The dynamics of police-citizen encounters with mentally ill persons. *Criminal Justice & Behavior, 43*(4), 459–482.

Schutt, R. K., & Goldfinger, S. M. (2011). *Homelessness, housing, and mental illness.* Cambridge, MA: Harvard University Press.

Scott, J., & Carrington, P. J. (2011). *The SAGE handbook of social network analysis.* Thousand Oaks, CA: SAGE Inc.

Scott, R. L. (2000). Evaluation of a mobile crisis program: Effectiveness, efficiency, and consumer satisfaction. *Psychiatric Services, 51*(9), 1153–1156.

Sellers, C. L., Sullivan, C. J., Veysey, B. M., & Shane, J. M. (2005). Responding to persons with mental illnesses: Police perspectives on specialized and traditional practices. *Behavioral Sciences and the Law, 23,* 647–657. doi:10.1002/bsi.633

Skeem, J. L., Manchak, S., & Peterson, J. K. (2011). Correctional policy for offenders with mental illness: Creating a new paradigm for recidivism research. *Law and Human Behavior, 35,* 110–126.

Slate, R. N., Buffington-Vollum, J. K., & Johnson, W. W. (2013). *The criminalization of mental illness: Crisis and opportunity for the justice system* (2nd ed.). Durham, NC: Academic University Press.

Steadman, H. J., Cocozza, J. J., & Veysey, B. M. (1999). Comparing outcomes for diverted and nondiverted jail detainees with mental illnesses. *Law and Human Behavior, 23*(6), 615–627.

Steadman, H. J., Deane, M. W., Borum, R., & Morrissey, J. P. (2000). Comparing outcomes of major models of police responses to mental health emergencies. *Psychiatric Services, 51*(5), 645–649.

Steadman, H. J., Osher, F. C., Robins, P. C., & Samuels, S. (2009). Prevalence of serious mental illness among jail inmates. *Psychiatric Services, 60*(6), 761–764. doi:10.1176/ps.2009.60.6.761

Stewart, J., & Ayres, R. (2001). Systems theory and policy practice: An exploration. *Policy Sciences, 34*, 79–94.

Substance Abuse and Mental Health Services Administration (SAMHSA). (2018). *Behavioral health services information system series: National directory of mental health treatment facilities.* Rockville, MD: Substance Abuse and Mental Health Services Administration.

Swartz, M. S., Swanson, J. W., Hiday, V. A., Borum, R., Wagner, R., & Burns, B. J. (1998). Violence and severe mental illness: The effects of substance abuse and nonadherence to medication. *The American Journal of Psychiatry, 155*(2), 226–231.

Taheri, S. A. (2016). Do crisis intervention teams reduce arrests and improve officer safety? A systematic review and meta-analysis. *Criminal Justice Policy Review, 27*(1), 76–96.

Teller, J. L. S., Munetz, M. R., Gil, K. M., & Ritter, C. (2006). Crisis intervention team training for police officers responding to mental disturbance calls. *Psychiatric Services, 57*(2), 232–237.

Thelander, B. L. (1997). The psychotherapy of Hildegard Peplau in the treatment of people with serious mental illness. *Perspectives in Psychiatric Care, 33*(3), 24–32.

Thompson, M. D., Reuland, M., & Souweine, D. (2003). Criminal justice/mental health consensus: Improving responses to people with mental illness. *Crime & Delinquency, 49*(1), 30–51.

Thornton, L. K., Baker, A. L., Lewin, T. J., Kay-Lambkin, F. J., Kavanagh, D., Richmond, R., Kelly, B., & Johnson, M. P. (2012). Reasons for substance use among people with mental disorders. *Addictive Behaviors, 37*, 427–434. doi:10.1016.j.addbeh.2011.11.039

Tiffany, F. (1890). *Life of Dorothea Lynde Dix.* Cambridge, MA: Higginson Book Company.

Torrey, E. (2010). Documenting the failure of deinstitutionalization. *Psychiatry, 73*(2), 122–124.

Torrey, E. F., Kennard, A. D., Eslinger, D., Lamb, R., & Pavle, J. (2010). *More mentally ill persons are in jail and prisons than hospitals: A survey of the states.* Arlington, VA: Treatment Advocacy Center and National Sheriffs Association.

Varelius, J. (2009). Defining mental disorder in terms of our goals for demarcating mental disorder. *Philosophy, Psychiatry, & Psychology, 16*(1), 32–52.

Vaughan, A. (2011, November). *Policing the mentally ill: A systems theory approach.* Paper presented at the annual meeting of the American Society of Criminology, Washington, D.C. Abstract retrieved from citation.allacademic.com/meta/p_mla_apa_research-citation/5/2/3/8/0/p523803_index.html

Vinkers, D. J., de Beurs, E., Barendregt, M., Rinne, T., & Hoek, H. W. (2011). The relationship between mental disorders and different types of crime. *Criminal Behaviour and Mental Health, 21*(5), 307–320.

Vogel, M., Stephens, K. D., & Siebels, D. (2014). Mental illness and the criminal justice system. *Sociology Compass, 8*(6), 627–638. doi:10.1111/soc4.12174

Wakefield, J. C. (1992). Disorder as harmful dysfunction: A conceptual critique of DSM-III-R's definition of mental disorder. *Psychological Review, 99*(2), 232–247.

Walker, S. (1994). *Sense and nonsense about crime and drugs: A policy guide.* Belmont, CA: Wadsworth Publishing Company.

Watson, A. C., Angell, B., Vidalon, T., & Davis, K. (2010). Measuring perceived procedural justice and coercion among persons with mental illness in police encounters: The police contact experience scale. *Journal of Community Psychology, 38*(2), 206–226. doi:10.1002/jcop.20360

Watson, A. C., Morabito, M. S., Draine, J., & Ottati, V. (2008). Improving police response to persons with mental illness: A multi-level conceptualization of CIT. *International Journal of Law and Psychiatry, 31*(4), 359–368. doi:10.1016/j.ijlp.2008.06.004

White, M. C., Chafetz, L., Collins-Bride, G., & Nickens, J. (2006). History of arrest, incarceration and victimization in community-based severely mentally ill. *Journal of Community Health, 31*, 123–135.

World Health Organization. (2011). *Investing in mental health.* Geneva, Switzerland: WHO Library Cataloguing-in-Publication Data.

Wyatt v. Stickney. (1972). 344 F. *Supp, 373*, 344.

Index

About the Authors

Kayla G. Jachimowski, PhD, is an assistant professor of Criminology, Law, & Society at Saint Vincent College in Latrobe, PA. Her primary areas of research include the intersection of mental health and the criminal justice system, and statistical methodology in criminological research.

Jonathon A. Cooper received his doctorate in criminology and criminal justice from Arizona State University in 2012. He is currently an associate professor at Indiana University of Pennsylvania in the Department of Criminology and Criminal Justice.

Made in the USA
Monee, IL
25 January 2023

26213514R00075